SPALDING®

Answers
to
Baseball's
Most
Asked
Questions

A. Lou Vickery

MASTERS PRESS

A Division of Howard W. Sams & Co.

Masters Press (A Division of Howard W. Sams & Co.)
2647 Waterfront Parkway, East Drive, Suite 300
Indianapolis, IN 46214

Library of Congress Cataloging-in-Publication Data

Vickery, A. Lou, 1941-
    Answers to baseball's most asked questions /
    A. Lou Vickery.
      p. cm.
    At head of title: Spalding
      ISBN: 1-57028-022-3: $12.95
      1. Baseball – Miscellanea.
      I. Title.   II. Title: Spalding answers to baseball's most asked
questions

GV867.3.V52   1995
796.357--dc20

             94-45936
             CIP

Credits:
Cover design by Kelli Ternet
Graphics by Phil Velikan
Edited by Kim Heusel and Heather Seal
Text layout by Kim Heusel

Table of Contents

Credits:
Cover photo by Joseph Arcure

Who's on First? by Bud Abbott and Lou Costello; from *Naughty Nineties*, Universal City Studios, 1945.

Introduction

A. Lou Vickery

New York Yankees: 1965 Spring Training

Many gray hairs ago I pitched baseballs for a living. I spent nine seasons in the St. Louis Cardinals, New York Yankees and Cincinnati Reds organizations. While I am no longer active in baseball, I remain close to the game.

Drawing on my experience as a player, coach and fan, this book answers some of your most frequently asked questions about baseball as well as some that may have not occurred to you. This book arose out of a conviction that there may be things you have observed in the past about baseball, but didn't quite understand. I believe you would like to talk more intelligently about how to "set up a hitter," how to hit behind the runner, and when and why a pitching change is needed. I think you want to get more pleasure out of watching baseball.

As you read, one thing you will find out quickly about baseball is there is more to the game than meets the bat. It's truly a very simple, yet complex game. The simplicity of baseball is wrapped up in see Tom throw, see Dick hit, see Harry run, see Bob field, see Bill catch.

Something special can be said for this simple version of baseball. One of the good things about being a baseball fan is that you don't have to be an expert. If you have a handle on a few of the fundamentals, know some of the basic rules and have some background on individual players, you can enjoy watching the game.

But there is more — much more — to baseball for those fans who really want to get into the game. Just enough of the complexity of the game rises above the surface to let any fan know that there is more for those willing to look and explore.

This book goes below the surface to explore some of the complexities found in the strategy, tactics and underlying skills. Regardless of the level you want to understand baseball, *ANSWERS TO BASEBALL'S MOST ASKED QUESTIONS* will make baseball a more easily understood and enjoyable game for you. And that makes this experience rewarding for both of us.

1
At Bat

What had been a quiet, but significant change in baseball toward greater offensive play has suddenly picked up speed. Run production in the mid-90s is up dramatically, baseballs are flying out of ballparks and runs are being scored at a record pace.

Experts most frequently list the following reasons for this sudden change:

- *"JUICED" OR LIVELIER BALLS.* Test results show that the ball has remained a constant for more than 50 years (see Chapter 9, page 106 for more details on the ball). But some feel the balls are harder and have higher seams. The higher seams add to the ball's rotation which keeps it in the air longer.

- *LACK OF QUALITY PITCHING.* There is little disagreement that pitching staffs have been diluted by expansion. The weaknesses on many major-league pitching staffs make the long ball a very formidable offensive weapon. In my day, pitchers were the best athletes. Today, the best athletes play offensive-oriented positions during their school years because that's where the glamour and the money are.

- *A SMALLER STRIKE ZONE.* According to the rule book, the strike zone covers the area from the top of the knees to the letters across the chest. Although umpires deny it, that area is much smaller in reality. A pitch above the belt is a certain ball, and the "low" strike seems to be several inches above the knees. If this is true, the hitters have a definite advantage.

- **ILLEGAL BATS.** Many contend that the corked bat is back (See page 10 in this chapter). Wholesale use of illegal bats is highly questionable, but a few hitters may be getting better results using them.

- **STRONGER HITTERS.** Hitters are bigger, stronger and quicker today because most of them spend hours in the weight room to get that way. This has an intimidating effect on weaker pitching staffs.

- **BETTER PLATE COVERAGE.** Hitters have become better at hitting pitches on both sides of the strike zone. As a result, more of them are "going with the pitch." Because of their improved strength training methods, many are strong enough to hit it out of the park to the opposite field.

- **PITCHERS FAIL TO PITCH INSIDE.** The tendency of hitters to become upset on a close inside pitch plays on pitchers. Fearing retaliation, many pitchers fail to make the inside pitch off the plate. For most hitters, this is an inviting pitch. When hitters no longer fear the high inside pitch, it becomes easier for them to stride and reach the pitch on the outside corner.

- **NEW PARKS ARE HITTER-FRIENDLY.** With fences easier to reach, pitchers are pitch "scared" and rely more on breaking balls. This increases the possibilities of handing curves or sliders which are a hitter's dream.

- **ARTIFICIAL PLAYING SURFACES.** Ground balls travel faster on artificial surface, increasing the chances for balls hit between the outfielders, resulting in extra-base hits (See page 8 of this chapter).

- **ENHANCED RUNNING GAMES.** A running strategy (straight steal, hit-and-run and other running-type plays) opens holes in the defense. When the runner starts on the pitch, it triggers movement by the infielders as they attempt to anticipate and adjust. It may work, but a well-executed running game often creates bigger holes within the inner defense that hitters can take advantage of.

There are numerous theories behind increased run production. The reality, however, is that alterations in hitting styles have modified the game. In this chapter, we take a closer look at some hitting skills and strategies — both physical and mental.

WHY IS HITTING A BASEBALL CALLED "ONE OF THE MOST DIFFICULT OF ALL ATHLETIC FEATS?"

To understand why, we only have to look at the two pieces of equipment basic to the game: the bat and ball. Both are round, yet, the objective is to hit the ball squarely. In other words, successful hitting requires two round objects that produce a square.

With that bit of brilliancy, we could probably stop right now in attempting to understand why hitting a baseball squarely and consistently is such a difficult task. But there are other reasons — most notably the pitcher.

The pitcher takes his windup, turns his body, kicks his leg high and takes his stride, carefully concealing the ball from the hitter. Not until the pitcher's arm comes forward to deliver the pitch to the plate does the hitter get his first good look at the ball.

Then, before the hitter knows it, the pitch, streaking to the plate at speeds around 90 mph, is upon him. He has less than one-half second to make two decisions: whether or not to swing, and, if he decides to swing, where to swing.

If he decides to swing, the hitter must bring the bat around at about 80 mph to meet the ball in exactly the right spot. Adding to the batter's difficulty, the ball is in reach of his bat for only about 1/50th of a second.

If all pitches came toward the plate at about the same speed and trajectory, hitting would be much easier. But the guy on the pitcher's mound has other ideas. To keep the hitter off balance, he changes the speed of his pitches, and throws curveballs, sliders and other pitches that change the ball's trajectory. The pitcher uses all the skill and cunning at his disposal to prevent a batter from hitting the ball squarely or with any authority. If the batter does hit the ball, the pitcher has the advantage of eight well-positioned fielders behind him to put the batter out.

With this in mind, it's not difficult to understand why even a hitter is unsuccessful 70-75 percent of the time — and still earn millions of dollars. That's why hitters have been called "successful failures."

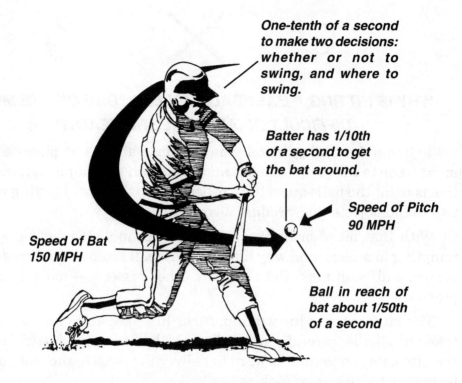

One-tenth of a second to make two decisions: whether or not to swing, and where to swing.

Batter has 1/10th of a second to get the bat around.

Speed of Pitch 90 MPH

Speed of Bat 150 MPH

Ball in reach of bat about 1/50th of a second

WHAT IS THE BATTER'S "HITTING ZONE?"

The "hitting zone" is a portion of the strike zone where the batter feels he has the best chance of getting "good wood" on the ball. The hitting zone can change from pitch to pitch, as well as from pitcher to pitcher. A good hitter will base his hitting zone on three things: game situation, the type of pitcher he is facing and the score.

On the first pitch, the batter may choose a 1-foot square area from his waist down across the heart of the plate as a hitting zone. This means he'll swing only at a pitch in this zone. He won't swing at a pitch out of this zone even if it results in a called strike.

If the batter takes the pitch for a first strike or fouls the pitch off, the hitting zone expands to include a greater portion of the strike zone. If the first pitch is a ball, the hitting zone is likely to remain the same until the first strike is recorded.

With two strikes, the entire strike zone becomes the hitting zone. It is worth noting that with a two-strike count, most hitters "shorten up a bit" or cut down on their swing in order to make more consistent contact with the ball. As a result, hitters who shorten up with two strikes don't strike out as often, but lose power in their swing.

A good hitter has the discipline to swing only at pitches in his hitting zone. Laying off pitches outside of his hitting zone makes it more likely he'll get a good pitch to hit. In this manner, he plays to his strengths — he uses the part of the strike zone where he feels he can be most successful.

THE HITTING ZONE

TWO STRIKES

ONE STRIKE

NO STRIKES

WHAT ROLE DOES THE TYPE OF BAT PLAY IN HITTING?

Most players use bats that weigh 32-38 ounces and are 32-36 inches long. Many players prefer a 34- or 35-inch, and a 33- or 34-ounce bat. Home run-type hitters sometimes prefer a 36-inch bat with a thin handle which provides more leverage, however. The thin handle makes it easier to "whip" the bat since most of the bat's weight is concentrated in its thicker upper area. By gripping the bat at the very end, the power hitter generates more bat speed.

The speed of the swing, and the length and force of the bat that moves through the swing into the ball determine how hard and how far the ball is hit. By contrast, a singles-type hitter may prefer a bat with a thick handle, giving him more hitting surface over the length of the bat. It also enables him to wait longer and still get good wood on the inside pitch to the opposite field, that is, the field opposite his natural hitting side at home plate (right field for a right-handed hitter). By being a little late on the swing, this kind of hitter can be more selective in the pitches he attempts to hit.

It's worth noting that all bats used at the professional level are still made of wood. Aluminum bats, used almost exclusively at all levels of amateur play, are taboo in the pros. Tradition has as much to do with this decision as does the increased chance for injury because of the speed the ball jumps off the aluminum bat.

Thin Handle Bat

WHAT PART DOES A BATTER'S STANCE PLAY IN HITTING?

A batter may stand deep in the batter's box or close to the plate. He may be almost erect, slightly bent or in a crouched position. His hands may be high off the ear, about shoulder level or down around his armpits. His weight may be evenly balanced over both legs or slightly over the rear leg.

What this amounts to is stances are about as individual as the players who use them. There are no hard and fast rules about a batter's stance except that he be comfortable, balanced, free of tension and capable of reaching all areas of the plate with his swing.

There are three types of foot placement in a batter's stance — open, parallel or closed. This is how they differ and what their advantages are.

Open. The front foot is placed farther from home plate than the rear foot. Hitters use the open stance because they can see the ball better and it's easier to pull the ball. Using this stance, however, makes it more difficult to get the weight onto the balls of the feet, which is necessary for adjusting to different kinds of pitches.

Parallel. This stance is favored by most hitters. The feet are approximately the same distance from the plate. Hitters are in a more balanced position to go with the pitch, and it provides for more consistent plate coverage.

Closed. The front foot is closer to the plate. Most batters who use the closed stance will stand deep in the box and away from the plate, and normally hit the ball with authority to the opposite field since they are pointed in that direction.

The three stances look something like this (right-handed hitter):

WHAT DOES IT MEAN WHEN IT IS SAID THAT GOOD HITTERS "LOOK FOR PITCHING PATTERNS?"

Good hitters study pitchers and know that pitchers throw in patterns. The habits of each individual pitcher will differ and may vary from game to game, but most pitchers will go to certain pitches in certain situations. This is especially true when they are in a tight spot with the game on the line. By studying each pitcher, hitters establish a "book" on what the pitchers like to throw and when they are likely to throw it.

They pay special attention to what type of pitch the pitcher prefers to use as a "cripple pitch," a pitch where the batter is ahead in the ball-strike count, 2-0 or 3-1. Unless his fastball is exceptional, a good pitcher probably will stay away from that pitch in this situation.

What the hitter studies in these situations is the type of pitch that is more apt to be thrown. Does he prefer a breaking ball — curve or slider — or is a change-up his favorite in these situations? When the hitter is ahead in the count, he can "sit on a pitch" (see the next question) or look for a certain pitch in his hitting zone.

WHAT IS A BATTER DOING WHEN HE IS "SITTING ON A PITCH?"

Most hitters "look" now and then for the pitcher to throw a certain type of pitch in a certain location. It could occur on the first pitch, but most often happens when the hitter is ahead in the count. In this situation, a batter can afford to sit on a pitch since he has an advantage over the pitcher.

If the batter gets the pitch he's looking for, he will probably be able to get a good swing at it. If he doesn't get "his pitch," he doesn't have to swing since he was ahead in the count. Some hitters will anticipate the pitch and its location until they have two strikes. Some go all the way through the third strike, especially if they are facing a particularly tough pitcher.

Today, most pitchers have four or five different pitches they can throw for strikes. Obviously, this changes the odds on which pitch to "sit on," but as long as the hitter is ahead in the count, he can afford to look for a certain pitch. If he gets it, the pitcher will probably pay for it.

WHAT ARE THE ADVANTAGES IN BEING A SWITCH-HITTER?

A hitter capable of batting from both the right and left sides of home plate has a distinct advantage: most of the pitcher's breaking pitches (curves, sliders, etc.) come into him, rather than break away from him. This gives him a better look at the pitch as it breaks. Consequently, he should experience better success in hitting the breaking pitch.

Some natural right-handed hitters with exceptional speed learn to hit left-handed to take advantage of their speed. Batting from the left side of the plate against a right-handed pitcher puts the speedy hitter about 2^1/$_2$ feet closer to first base.

The swing from the left side also carries the batter toward first base. This is not the case when hitting from the right side: the swing carries the right-handed batter's body toward third base. As a result, the left-handed batter gains nearly 4 feet and one-fourth of a second going to first base — often the difference between being out or safe in a close play.

Players with the ability to switch-hit are at a premium. Ballclubs with several switch-hitters can carry one more pitcher and one less fielder because the manager doesn't have to pinch-hit for the switch-hitter in normal left versus left, or right versus right pitcher-to-hitter situations.

HOW DOES AN ARTIFICIAL PLAYING FIELD AFFECT HITTING?

Artificial playing surfaces put the accent on speed for both the ball and the hitter. The odds of getting a base hit improve on an artificial surface because of the over-spin the harder surface creates on ground balls.

Infielders must play a step or two deeper to compensate for the ball's increased speed on the artificial turf. This aids the speedy hitter who is adept at bunting and those who can hit down on the pitch to create opportunities for infield hits. Outfielders also must play deeper to keep base hits from getting in the gaps between them and going to the fence. This increases the chances a short fly ball or soft line drive will drop in for a hit.

The heat of summer also favors the hitter on artificial surface. The turf doesn't absorb the heat, making it much hotter on the field. Heat takes it toll on pitchers, causing them to tire faster and more easily.

About the only detriment to batting on artificial surfaces comes when a sacrifice bunt is in order. The hard surface makes it difficult for the bunter to "deaden" the ball, decreasing the chances of success.

For the record, to bunt successfully on an artificial surface, the bunter must make sure the bunt hits the dirt area in front of home plate before it reaches the artificial turf. The dirt will deaden the ball, giving the runner precious time in moving up a base while the fielder makes the play on the ball.

WHY IS A GROUND BALL TO THE SECOND BASEMAN CALLED "THE MOST UNDERRATED PLAY IN BASEBALL?"

A hitter with a runner on second base and no one out in a close game is expected "to give himself up" and take a shot at right field. In this situation the batter attempts to hit the pitch on the ground toward the right side of the infield to advance the runner to third where he is in a better position to score.

In this situation, nearly every hitter in the lineup is expected to take at least one swing with the idea of hitting the ball toward right field. Most will be asked to attempt to move the runner to third until there are two strikes. A runner on third is in position to score on a fly ball, passed ball, wild pitch, error or any number ways other than those available at second base. That's why the ground ball to second base may be the most underrated play in baseball, but one of the most important.

There are three reasons why taking a shot at right field also has merit when there is a runner on first base with less than two outs:

1) The first baseman is holding the runner on, which leaves a bigger hole to hit through.

2) Chance for a double play are reduced when the ball is hit to the second baseman's left.

3) If the ball goes through for a base hit, the runner has an excellent chance of ending up on third base.

WHY DO HOME-RUN HITTERS SEEM TO STRIKE OUT MORE THAN OTHER PLAYERS?

There are three reasons for this:

1) They must quickly make up their minds to swing.

2) The head of the bat must travel a greater distance.

3) The swing must be harder.

Most long-ball hitters try to meet the ball 12-18 inches in front of home plate which requires a quick decision on whether or not to swing. The bat head also must cover a greater distance at a quicker pace but still make contact with the ball in a very small area.

This increases the margin of error. The only way the batter can get the bat head out in front is to swing hard, and the harder the swing, the more vulnerable he is to curves, sliders and off-speed pitches resulting in more strikeouts.

WHAT IS A "CORKED" BAT? WHY IS IT ILLEGAL?

Tampering or altering a bat in any form or fashion is illegal. Some hitters resort to inserting cork or rubber in their bats to increase bat speed and generate more power. The bat feels lighter, which is an added psychological advantage.

Corking a bat is accomplished in this manner:

1) A 1-inch diameter hole is drilled 6-8 inches deep into the barrel end of the bat.

2) Glue is poured into the hole to act as a sealer.

3) Cork shavings or rubber balls are packed tightly into the hole to act as a springboard for the ball when it is hit.

4) A dowel is wedged into the hole opening, compressing the material.

5) To cover evidence of tampering, the top of the bat is sanded smooth and a darkening substance is rubbed over the sanded area.

6) Finally, the tampered end of the bat is scuffed and banged on a rough surface to cover up the alterations.

If a fair ball is hit with an illegal bat, and the bat is discovered to be illegal, the hitter may be suspended for period determined by the league president.

WHAT TIPS WILL THE BATTING COACH OFFER A HITTER WHO IS IN A SLUMP?

If we moved to the batting cage and listened to the hitting coach as he worked with a hitter in a slump, here are some things we would hear:

"DRIVE YOUR FRONT SHOULDER." To be a good hitter, a player must make an aggressive movement with his front shoulder back toward the pitcher as he swings the bat. This is important because the front shoulder leads the swing. If the front shoulder rotates out too quickly, the head and body are sure to follow resulting in 1) the batter failing to keep his eye on the ball, and 2) reducing the amount of body weight behind the swing.

"EXTEND YOUR ARMS." If the momentum and power generated by the batter's swing are to pay dividends, the arms should be fully extended at the point of contact between bat and ball. Without this extension, the ball will not be hit very hard or very far.

"GO BACK." As the pitcher prepares to deliver the pitch, the batter's weight is divided evenly over both legs in a balanced stance. Upon the release of the pitch, the batter shifts his weight to the back leg as he initiates the stride forward with his front leg. The hitting coach reminds the batter to "go back" in order to properly go forward. That is, unless the batter transfers his weight to his back leg, he will be unable to put his whole body into the swing as he goes forward into the pitch.

"HIT IT BACK AT THE PITCHER." When a batter has been in a slump for a few games, the hitting coach will tell him to try to hit the ball back toward the pitcher. This mentality gives the batter a much better chance to make more consistent contact because he watches the ball better and improves his mechanics as he swings the bat.

"KEEP THOSE HANDS BACK." This is what the hitting coach shouts out to the batter who commits his hands too early in the swing. A hitter can wait slightly longer and be more selective if he keeps his hands back just off the tip of his rear shoulder until the front foot hits the ground on the stride. The hitter who commits his hands too quickly is easier to fool with a pitch and loses power in the process.

"OPEN YOUR HIPS." The outward rotation of the hips is important to a batter's power. "Opening the hips" permits the hands, wrists and momentum of the body to come forward freely, transferring weight forward into the swing. Opening the hips too quickly will also create a problem hitting the ball. Timing is truly the key in hitting and the actions of the hips are indicative of this importance.

"STAY BACK." This is for the hitter who rushes his swing to keep his weight on his rear leg as long as possible before shifting his weight to his front leg. In other words, if he moves his weight onto his front leg too quickly, he loses the effectiveness of the stride, causing him to be able to generate power only with his arms and wrists. The longer the batter can "stay back" the more body weight he has to put into the swing and the less likely he is to be fooled on a breaking or off-speed pitch.

"TUCK YOUR CHIN." Successful hitters watch the ball as long as possible. To accomplish this, the hitting coach will remind the batter to tuck his chin, a mental instruction to the batter to lower his head on the swing in order to keep his eye on the ball. As the chin goes down, so do the eyes.

"HIT IT OUT FRONT." The optimum position for making contact with the ball is anywhere from 2-18 inches in front of the plate. The closer the pitch is on the inside part of the plate, the further out the point of contact should be. Improvement in this action enables the hitter to 1) put the ball in play in fair territory, and 2) hit the breaking pitch before it really begins to break.

"HIT THROUGH THE BALL." This bit of batting instruction reminds the hitter who tends to stop his swing as soon as the bat makes contact with the ball to swing all the way through. The effect of each swing is maximized if a hitter completes the swing with a good follow-through by bringing the bat all the way around and "hitting through the ball."

"GET ON TOP OF THE BALL." This is for hitters who tend to uppercut (swing up from south to north) at the pitch. To counteract this tendency, the hitting coach will tell the hitter to "get on top of the ball" by swinging slightly downward. This has the effect of canceling out the tendency to uppercut, producing a level swing.

WHY DO LEFT-HANDED HITTERS HAVE MORE DIFFICULTY AGAINST LEFT-HANDED PITCHERS THAN RIGHT-HANDED HITTERS AGAINST RIGHT-HANDED PITCHERS?

The average left-handed hitter has more trouble with left-handed pitchers for one simple reason: he faces less of them. The left-handed hitter faces more right-handed pitchers. As a result, he may experience more difficulty when he does bat against one.

Platooning policies of many managers haven't helped the average left-handed hitter. From the time they set foot in the big leagues, many lefty swingers are benched when certain southpaws take to the mound. Here again, less exposure has led to fewer chances for improvement.

This question may eventually become a moot point as the number of left-handed pitchers and hitters increases. Managers will have little choice but to keep many of their better left-handed hitters in the lineup to face the slants of left-handed pitchers.

ARE MOST BATTERS AFRAID OF BEING HIT BY A PITCH?

Whether they admit it or not, the majority of hitters are scared of being hit by the ball. And for good reason. Even the pitchers with great control occasionally let a fastball slip or get misdirected, and when that happens, there's a good chance the batter will get hit. A baseball traveling 85-90 mph is going to hurt when it hits a human body. In some cases it can cause serious and even crippling injuries.

A batter is very much aware that at any time a pitcher can hit him, and that's a real psychological advantage for the pitcher. It weighs on the batter, who day after day faces this hazard. If he succumbs to his fear, it takes away his positive attitude and aggressiveness.

Most good hitters simply admit that the possibility of being hit exists — it's part of the game. They just handle it and move on. But hitters who have a reputation for allowing close pitches to affect their ability to hit can expect a lot of "purpose" pitches — pitches purposely thrown close to them with the intention of shaking them up.

Today, almost any close pitch — purpose or misdirected — brings the batter charging to the mound, ready to do physical battle with the pitcher. Retaliation seems to be the rule of the day.

2
On the
Bases

The home run is definitely in vogue. Weaknesses on many major-league pitching staffs make the home run a very formidable weapon, but there are clubs which try to manufacture runs rather than sit back and wait for a big inning.

There are several reasons some clubs have put more emphasis on their running games beginning with overall improvement in team speed followed by the bigger stadiums with their artificial surfaces which allow ground balls and line drives to find their way between the fielders. With greater speed at their disposal, managers are using the straight steal, hit-and-run and other running strategies more often to score runs.

Running has added importance on artificial surfaces where ground balls travel faster than on natural grass. Starting the runners as the pitcher releases the ball causes the infielders to move around creating bigger holes in the defense. With the added speed of the ball, it doesn't take much for a ground ball to get through the infield for a base hit.

In this chapter we will take a closer look at some the fundamentals — both physical and mental — of baserunning skills and strategies.

HOW DOES AN AGGRESSIVE BASERUNNING PHILOSOPHY PUT ADDITIONAL PRESSURE ON THE DEFENSE?

Clubs that regularly bunt, execute the hit-and-run and steal bases create situations that get the defense out of sync. Reputation has as much to do with this as anything. Clubs noted for an aggressive baserunning style have an element of threat working for them that's just as significant in making the defense lose its composure as the successful execution of the offensive play itself.

When playing a club that likes to run, the shortstop and second baseman play a little closer to second base to cover the base on steal or hit-and-run plays. That makes the holes between infielders a little bigger, and they get even larger when the first and third basemen play tighter to guard against a bunt attempt for a base hit.

Outfielders are also wary of daring baserunning. They are thinking, "If the ball is hit to me, I've got to charge it and hurry my throw," increasing the chances for a misplay or overthrow.

The pitcher and catcher also are in the act. The pitcher's attention is divided between the runner he knows is a threat to steal and the batter. The pitcher tells himself, "I've got to hold the runner close to the base. I've got to get the ball to the plate in a hurry." While concentrating on the runner, he serves up a fat pitch or falls behind in the ball-strike count.

The catcher calls for more fastballs in running situations because he can receive the pitch and get rid of it more quickly. The hitters have an advantage in this situation. All they do is keep looking for the fastball, because they know the odds are good that they will get one to hit.

Aggressive baserunning adds a vital dimension to most ballclubs. With the state of pitching today, teams need to manufacture as many runs as possible. By keeping the runners moving, managers put additional pressure on the defense increasing the chances of misplays and errors. But the bottom line on a sound baserunning strategy is that it helps win ballgames.

WHAT MAKES A GOOD BASE RUNNER?

There is no substitute for speed, but the speediest players aren't necessarily the best base runners. The mental side — knowledge of the opposition, of baserunning strategy and how to apply it on the base paths, and correct execution of baserunning skills — is an important factor in becoming a top-notch base runner.

This is possibly the least recognizable side of baserunning from our viewpoint in the stands. While players with speed may "outrun" some of their mental mistakes, a great base runner must master baserunning's mental equation.

The kind of information the better base runners have stored in their mental computers includes:

- Pickoff move of the pitcher
- Throwing arm and accuracy of the catcher
- Individual style of the second baseman and shortstop in making the pivot at second
- Which outfielders are slow or fast in charging the ball
- Which outfielders field the ball quickly and get it away in a hurry
- Throwing ability of each outfielder
- Type of hitter at the plate

Armed with this kind of information, base runners are less likely to commit mental errors while on the bases.

THERE ARE 11 MORE WAYS A RUNNER CAN SCORE FROM THIRD BASE THAN FROM SECOND. WHAT ARE THEY?

1 — infield out   **2** — infield hit   **3** — fly ball

4 — error   **5** — wild pitch   **6** — passed ball

7 — squeeze play   **8** — bases-loaded walk   **9** — balk

10 — steal of home   **11** — catcher's interference

WHAT MAKES A GOOD BASE STEALER?

The knowledge of his strengths as well as his limitations sets at the top of the list of what makes a good base stealer. More specifically, a good base stealer has above average to excellent speed, a broad knowledge of opposing pitchers, sound techniques on how to get a good jump and is great at sliding, an often-overlooked skill.

The bent-leg slide (following page) is the most commonly used by base runners. Bending the leg and tucking it under the other leg cushions the body's weight and provides instant mobility. The slider is able to spring up and go on to the next base in case of an erratic throw.

Bent-leg slide

WHY IS BEING THE FIRST OUT AT HOME PLATE A CARDINAL SIN OF BASERUNNING UNLESS IT'S THE RESULT OF A BASES-LOADED FORCE PLAY?

Two situations come to mind where being the first out at home most often occurs and causes the guilty player to draw the ire of his manager. The first is when the runner on second attempts to score and is thrown out at the plate. The second is when the runner on third tries to score on a ground ball to a drawn-in infield and becomes an easy out at home.

On the latter play, there is little doubt the runner made an error in judgment. Being thrown out attempting to score from second with no outs makes the third base coach the culprit unless the runner runs right through the coach's stop sign.

With no one out, the third base coach should have no doubt in his mind that the runner can score from second on a base hit before sending him home. With at least three chances to score the run, why run into a potential suicide play? Keep that in mind the next time you see the third base coach fail to send the runner when there are no outs and it appears the runner could walk home from third base.

WHY IS IT BAD BASERUNNING STRATEGY TO BE THE FIRST OR LAST OUT AT THIRD BASE?

Being thrown out trying to go from first to third base on a base hit when no one is out, or when two men are out, is poor baserunning strategy for several reasons. With no outs, the runner doesn't want to kill a potential rally by taking a chance. Obviously, a base runner is in a better scoring position on third base than second, but with no outs, the gamble of going to third doesn't warrant the risk.

When there are two outs, the runner is only slightly better off at third than second. From third he can score on a wild pitch, passed ball, balk, error, etc. But in most cases, it takes a base hit to score him — a hit that most likely would have scored him from second base. With these odds, he serves his club just well at second as third.

What about with one out? If a runner is going to try to go from first to third on a batted ball to the outfield, this is the best time to do it. At third with one out he's in position to score on a fly ball or ground out — ways in which his run would not count if there were two outs.

WHAT DOES IT MEAN TO "NEVER RUN YOURSELF INTO AN OUT?"

A smart baserunning decision is never to "run yourself into an out." The occasion this is likely to happen is with a runner on first base with less than two outs and a slow ground ball is hit directly to the second baseman. Since the ball is not hit hard enough for a second-to-short-to-first double play, the second baseman will attempt to tag the oncoming runner and relay the ball to first base for the double play.

The smart runner will stop before reaching the area where the second baseman fields the ball, forcing him to field the ball and run toward the base runner for the tag. This should allow enough time for the batter to safely reach first base.

WHAT ARE THE PRIMARY DUTIES
OF THE THIRD BASE COACH?

The third base coach has many duties:

- He gives the signs to the batter and the base runner.
- If there is a runner on second, he keeps a close watch on the second baseman and shortstop, advising the runner if a pick-off play is attempted.
- On a base hit with a runner on second, or on an extra-base hit with a runner on first, he must decide whether or not to send the runner home.
- When there is a base hit to right field, he will instruct the runner on first to stop at second or continue to third.

These are the visible duties that are on display for all to see. But it's what we can't see — the great store of knowledge and information about the opposing club, the game situation, the abilities of his base runners, combined with his own ability to sort out this information and make instantaneous decisions — that measures the true value of a third base coach.

His decisions are no better than the knowledge and information he has at his disposal. The kind of information and knowledge a third base coach has stored in his mental computer includes:

- Strength and accuracy of the throwing arms of the opposing outfielders
- The outfielders' speed in getting to the ball
- Strength and accuracy of the infielders' throwing arms on relay plays
- Speed and baserunning skills of the runner(s) on base
- Hitting ability of the on-deck batter

This information, coupled with knowledge of the actual game situation — positioning of the outfielders, where the ball is hit, number of outs and the score — helps the coach make his decisions.

WHAT IS THE THIRD BASE COACH'S TOUGHEST DECISION IN ASSISTING A BASE RUNNER?

The toughest decision for a third base coach is deciding whether to send the runner home from second on a single or from first on an extra-base hit. In either situation, with less than two outs, the third base coach needs to be certain the runner can score on a base hit before sending him home. If the pitcher or slumping hitter is due to bat next, the coach might make an exception take a chance on a wild throw or a misplay.

The situation changes with two outs. The runner almost always will be sent home from second on a base hit with two outs because he is able to leave the base as soon as the ball is hit.

On potential scoring plays, the third base coach will leave the coach's box. The rules permit him to move out of the box toward home plate as long as he does not interfere with the play. Normally in this situation he will be midway between third and home facing the runner.

The coach moves up the line to keep the runner in front of him, enabling him to better assist the runner with visual signs since verbal instructions may not be heard over the noise of the crowd.

DON'T FANS BLAME THE THIRD BASE COACH FOR BASERUNNING BLUNDERS WHICH HE CAN'T CONTROL?

The third base coach does get blamed for baserunning mistakes which he really cannot control. For example, with one out, a runner is first and the game is tied, the batter singles to left-center field. The center fielder cuts the ball off and makes a strong, accurate throw to third base putting out the runner coming from first. In this situation, the decision to advance to third is the runner's, not the coach's. Since the play is in front of the runner, he can see it all the way. The decision is his alone.

The base runner on first uses the third base coach only when he must turn his head to the side to see the ball. He is on his own for all hits from right-center field to the left-field line. On base hits from straightaway right field to the right field line, the runner will look for the third base coach as he approaches second base. The coach will hold up his hands to tell the runner if he should stop at second or move his right arm in circular motion if should continue to third.

If the coach wants the runner to hold up and the runner continues to third base, the error is the runner's, not the coach's. If this happens, voice displeasure toward the runner, not the coach.

WHAT ARE THE FIRST BASE COACH'S PRIMARY DUTIES?

The duties of the first base coach are not as varied, or as crucial, as those of the third base coach. But they are still important.

The first base coach's duties begin as soon as the batter hits the ball. On a ground ball, the coach will let the batter-runner know if the ball goes through the infield by immediately yelling, "Make a turn." This means he wants the batter-runner to round the base and be in a position to go to second if the ball is misplayed in the outfield. He will also give a visual sign by extending both arms toward the infield.

On a ball hit fair down the left-field line, the coach may yell, "Go for two," meaning the runner should continue to second base. Normally, the batter-runner will pick up the ball with his eyes and decide for himself whether to try to make second. When the ball is behind the batter-runner down the left-field line, he depends on the coach's judgment.

As soon as the runner reaches first base, the coach will advise him where the ball is and to stay on the base until the pitcher takes his stretch position. This eliminates any chance of being put out by a "hidden ball" play.

The coach also reminds the runner of several things:

- The number of outs
- To look at the third base coach for a possible sign
- To check the positioning of the outfielders
- The pick-off move of the pitcher
- To make sure a line drive goes through the infield

3
Signs and Signals

One of the most intriguing parts of baseball is the elaborate, confidential communication system all ballclubs use. There is a simple reason clubs go to such lengths to devise a set of signs and signals — opponents would have an advantage if they knew what the other team planned to do. "Stealing" a sign at a crucial point in the game could be the difference between winning and losing.

A fun part of being at the ballpark is watching the third base coach giving the signs. Even the most perceptive fans know little about the complicated pattern of signals used to convey plays and plans between manager and the third base coach, third base coach and batter or base runner, and between player and player.

All clubs use a network in an effort to steal signs. Opposing clubs counter this espionage by constantly changing signs, and using camouflage and deception while signalling. Whether offensive or defensive, clubs devote a great deal of time going over signs and signals. This is done in clubhouse meetings before a series with each opponent. A ballclub's success depends on the confidentiality of its signs and signals.

WHY IS IT THE THIRD BASE COACH, NOT THE COACH AT FIRST BASE, WHO RELAYS SIGNALS TO THE BATTER AND/OR RUNNER?

Signals usually begin with the manager who gives the sign to the third base coach. This is the reason most home clubs occupy the first base dugout. Since he is looking directly into the dugout, the third base coach in a better position to see the signal and relay it to the appropriate player.

The first base coach would have to turn his body to see the sign, increasing the difficulty in picking it up and delaying its delivery to the hitters and runners.

The bottom line: the third base coach hastens the delivery of the signal. Any delay improves the opposition's chances to "steal" the sign or anticipate the play.

WHY DOES THE THIRD BASE COACH GO THROUGH SUCH GYRATIONS WHEN GIVING SIGNS TO BATTERS AND RUNNERS?

If the third base coach went through his actions only when a play was on, the defense would be alerted. This is the reason the coach is continually moving his arms and hands. Most of these motions are decoys meant to disguise the sign from the opponents.

The players' role in this acting job is to continue looking until the coach has completed his motions. If a player looks away too soon it would be a tip-off that the sign has been given and the rest of the motions are just decoys.

WHAT ARE SOME METHODS COACHES USE IN GIVING SIGNS?

There are as many different methods of giving signs as there are ballclubs. Through the years, most big-league teams have found "flash" and "block" signs are best. They can be given quickly and combine simplicity with camouflage, making them more difficult for opponents to "steal."

FLASH SIGNS

A flash sign is a particular action within a series of actions that signals a certain play is on. For example, suppose the signal for a bunt is rubbing the shirt with the right hand. To properly disguise the bunt sign, the third base coach might touch the bill of his cap with his left hand, rub his chin with his right hand, rub his shirt with his right hand (bunt sign), rub his right leg and clap his hands. All this action is done to camouflage the bunt sign.

Shown below is a complete set of flash signs.

- **Right hand to face** .... Take a pitch
- **Right hand to shirt** ....Bunt
- **Left hand to chin**..................................... Hit-and-run
- **Left hand to leg** .... Steal
- **Right hand to belt**... Squeeze
- **Left hand to cap bill** .... Double steal
- **Right hand to ear**........................... Take off any sign

By using a slightly more complicated method, the third base coach can further disguise flash signs. It involves the use of a key or indicator. Here's how the key is used.

Regardless of the sign the coach wants the player to receive, the sign isn't activated until the coach first touches something designated as the key. The next action is the one that counts.

If the left hand to the nose is the key, for example, and the coach wants the runner to receive the steal sign — left hand to leg, all movements are meaningless until the coach touches his nose with his left hand. Once he touches his key and immediately follows it with his left hand rubbing his leg, the steal sign is on. If the coach rubs his left leg prior to hitting his key it would mean nothing.

That's about as simple as signs get at the major-league level. From here, things can get even more complicated in efforts to keep the opposition guessing. Here are a few examples:

- A different set of flash signs may be used for each three innings of a game.
- With a right-handed hitter, only signs given with the right hand may apply. The same may be true for a left-handed hitter.
- In rare cases, each player may have a separate set of signs.

The inclusion of a take off sign — right hand to ear — adds to the deception. The take off sign is just what it implies — it takes off any previously given sign. Any time the coach touches his take off sign last, it means no sign is on.

Now, let's see what you have learned. Answer quickly using the set of signs previously described. Here's the third base coach's sequence: Left hand to shirt, right hand to cap bill, right hand to chin, left hand to nose, right hand to shirt, left hand down pants leg, right hand to ear. What's the play?

If you followed the procedure correctly, the answer is "Nothing." In this situation the coach put the bunt sign on when he went to his shirt with his right hand immediately after touching his key — left hand to nose. However, the last place he touched was the ear with his right hand — the take off sign, cancelling the sign that put a play on.

BLOCK SIGNS

This version of sign giving divides the body into blocks. For example: the head area is one block, the shirt area another and the pants area still another. The strategy behind block signs is to use each section of the body for a particular segment of the batting order:

- Head area for the first three hitters in the lineup
- Shirt area for the next three hitters
- Pants area for the last three hitters and all pinch hitters

In giving block signs, the third base coach will use rubs — the number of rubs determines the sign. The key factor is that the rubs must be in the block of the player who is receiving the sign.

For example, if the bunt is two rubs and the coach wants a hitter in the upper third of the batting order to bunt, he would rub some portion of his head area (cap included) twice.

As with flash signs, the coach goes through a series of movements while giving the block sign. With the first three hitters, he might rub his shirt and pants leg before going to his face to give the sign and then return to his leg for a rub or two. He will include the sign within a series of actions in order to better camouflage the signal.

It's important that the player receiving the sign continue to look at the coach until all movement is completed. To safeguard against the player looking away as soon as he receives the sign and risking tipping off the sign, most clubs make it a rule that the player continue to look until the coach gives him a "look-away" sign. This could be nothing more than the coach clapping his hands and glancing out toward the outfield. Only then should the player turn his attention away from the coach.

WHY DOES THE CATCHER NEED DIFFERENT SIGNS FOR THE PITCHER WHEN THERE IS A RUNNER ON SECOND BASE?

Through the years, the catcher's signs to the pitcher with no one on second base have been virtually the same: one finger for a fastball, two for a curveball, three for a slider, four if the pitcher has a special pitch and a wiggle of the fingers for a change-up (see Chapter 4 for further details on these pitches).

Once a runner reaches second base, it's necessary for the catcher to switch signals because the runner has the same vantage point as the pitcher. This puts the runner in a prime spot to steal the catcher's signs and relay them to the hitter.

Unless the catcher switches to a more complicated system, the runner can pick up the signs and flash a prearranged sign to the batter as to what pitch is being thrown. For example, a swinging right fist could be the runner's sign to the batter that the catcher has signaled for a fastball, hands on both knees could mean a breaking pitch, a tug at the cap may signal a change-up. (We take a closer look at this later in the chapter).

Most batters prefer to have knowledge of only one type of pitch. For instance, if the batter is a good fastball hitter, he may want to know only when the catcher has signalled a fastball. The batter can then "sit on" the fastball, figuring he will see at least one during this time at bat.

Even though stealing the catcher's signs is rarely done, stealing the sign for an expected pitch could prove the difference between winning or losing late in a close game. Throughout the game, runners who reach second base pass along information on the signs to a bench coach. The coach assimilates the data and tries to establish a pattern the catcher uses to signal the pitcher. When reasonably certain that a pattern exists, the coach passes the information to the players.

If the opposing pitcher suspects the runner of attempting to steal the signs, he might throw a high, hard fastball right under the batter's chin. In fact, this is the "equalizer" which keeps the stealing of the pitch signs by the runner on second to a minimum. Obviously, switching signs helps eliminate sign stealing, too.

WHAT ARE SOME OF THE VARIATIONS IN SIGNALS USED BY A CATCHER WITH A RUNNER ON SECOND?

There are many ways to switch signs, some that require the pitcher to be a mathematical whiz. For the most part, catchers try to use signs that are simple, yet effective, with a runner on second.

The simplest system is the flash set of signs similar to those given by the third base coach. Let's say, for example, that the catcher wants to call for a fastball and that the third sign flashed is the desired pitch. In this case, the catcher puts down one finger, then three fingers, then one finger again, then two fingers. Only the third flash, one finger, counts and that is the fastball sign.

A much more complicated system is the multiple-digit method used by clubs with a history of stealing signs, or on occasions when a crafty veteran is camped on second base. It works this way:

Suppose the pitcher has four pitches in his repertoire — *fastball (1)*, *curve (2), slider (3)* and *change-up (4).* In this case, the pitcher will add in multiples of four. The catcher puts down one finger first, followed by two fingers, then three fingers for a total of six numbers. Once the pitcher's count reaches four, he starts over and adds after four. This leaves him at two — six minus four — the curveball sign.

Now that you have figured it out, want to give it try? The catcher shows in quick sequence one finger, three fingers and one finger again for a total of five. What's the call? It was easy, wasn't it? Fastball. But it's not quite that easy when you are on the mound with a one-run lead and facing the cleanup hitter with runners on second and third.

Because of the intense concentration pitching requires, pitchers prefer the simplest signs. They don't want to waste mental energy trying to decipher complicated formulas.

WHEN WATCHING GAMES ON TV, THE CATCHER MAY BE SEEN GIVING A SET OF SIGNS FOLLOWED BY AN OUTWARD MOVEMENT OF THE HAND. WHAT KIND OF SIGNAL IS THIS?

When the TV camera zooms in on the catcher giving the signs, occasionally you will see the catcher actually giving two signals to the pitcher. One is for the desired pitch and the other is for the desired location of the pitch.

For a right-handed hitter, for example, the catcher puts down one finger for a fastball and follows by motioning with his hand toward his left leg. Here he is indicating that he wants the pitch thrown on the inside part of the plate. Conversely, if he motions toward his other leg, he wants the ball delivered out and away from the hitter.

At other times, the catcher signals for the desired pitch, then motions with his hand either up or down. The upward motions indicate he wants the pitch to be thrown high in the strike zone. A downward movement indicates he wants the pitch down and probably out of the strike zone.

The catcher's signal for the location of the pitch is a mental jog for the pitcher. It is the catcher's way of emphasizing the importance of making sure the pitcher concentrates on hitting a certain spot. Catchers tend to specify pitch location to pitchers known to lose their concentration from time to time.

WITH A RUNNER ON FIRST BASE, HOW DO THE SHORTSTOP AND SECOND BASEMAN DECIDE WHO COVERS SECOND ON AN ATTEMPTED STEAL OR HIT-AND-RUN PLAY?

The next time you are at a game, observe the shortstop when there is a runner on base. It's his job to signal to the second baseman which player will cover the bag on an attempted steal or hit-and-run play.

Just before the pitch, the shortstop will shield his mouth with his glove and give the second baseman the cover sign. An open mouth could mean the shortstop will cover. A closed mouth could mean the second baseman will cover.

The decision as to which one of the middle infielders will cover on a steal or hit-and-run attempt is based on the game situation, the base runner, the hitter at the plate, the pitcher, the ball-strike count and the pitch that has been called. Since both the shortstop and second baseman can see the catcher's signal to the pitcher, the cover sign is given by the shortstop immediately after he sees the catcher's sign. The expected pitch has a bearing on where the ball might be hit, so the shortstop waits until he has all the data before making his call. His call of who covers may vary from pitch to pitch, too.

The reason the shortstop shields his mouth is that he does not want the hitter to know who is covering. A hitter who can handle the bat can guide the ball into a hole vacated by a covering infielder if he knows who is covering the base.

AFTER A BATTER REACHES FIRST BASE WITH LESS THAN TWO OUTS, WHY DOES THE PITCHER GLANCE AT THE SHORTSTOP BEFORE PITCHING TO THE NEXT HITTER?

When the possibility of a pitcher-to-second-to-first double play exists, the shortstop will inform the pitcher as to who will be covering second base. The shortstop does this with a prearranged signal.

It may be nothing more than the shortstop pointing his finger toward the pitcher and then toward himself, but this doesn't necessarily mean that the shortstop is covering. The reverse could be true. The shortstop could point a finger at himself which would mean the second baseman is covering. Conversely, if the shortstop points his finger at the second baseman, that means he (the shortstop) is covering on a ground ball back to the pitcher.

Why all this cloak-and-dagger stuff just to let the pitcher know who is covering the base? Because the hitter also wants to know who's covering. This is especially true of the hitter who can spray the ball to different fields and play hit-and-run.

Even though the infielder covering the base on a ground ball back to the pitcher may differ from the one who covers on an attempted steal or hit-and-run play, the odds lean toward the same infielder covering on all plays for that particular batter. The smart hitter will look for who is covering and attempt to hit the ball on a hit-and-run into the hole left by the fielder moving to cover the base. Occasionally, the batter will make an incorrect guess, but he likes the odds over the long haul.

HOW DOES THE CLUB IN THE FIELD TRY TO STEAL THE OFFENSIVE TEAM'S SIGNS?

Stealing the opposition's signs is a vital part of baseball. All clubs practice this form of thievery. Through the years, some players have been able to extend their big-league careers because of their exceptional ability in pilfering signs.

When on defense, players on the field, as well as those on the bench are alert to opportunities to steal signs. The major thrust of the espionage, however, generally revolves around a couple of players on the bench.

Their thievery naturally begins by watching the manager of the opposing club who starts the sign-giving process by giving the sign to the third base coach. But stealing signs in this manner is difficult because of all the activity in the opposing dugout. Their best bet is to turn their attention to the third base coach, the base runner and/or batter who are out in the open and much easier to observe.

Sign larceny works best with the buddy system. One player or coach on the bench watches the coach, while a second keeps his eyes on the runner or hitter. Sitting side by side in the dugout, they coordinate four eyes in an effort to decode the third base coach's signs. Focusing simultaneously on the coach and either the batter or base runner, the two players will deliver a running commentary on the actions of the respective parties. If they pick up something that indicates they possibly have stolen a sign, they will confirm it before alerting their own catcher. Once confirmation is made, the catcher will be alerted by a prearranged verbal signal.

By now you may be wondering why a running commentary between players is needed to try to decipher the opposition's signs. Why watch the runner or hitter, you might ask? Why not just watch the third base coach?

The key to unraveling the sign puzzle is not found in figuring out the method used by the coach to give the signs. Even the exceptionally talented spy has difficulty decoding all the movements and actions of the coach. Therefore, when a sign is stolen, it is the actions of the runner and/or the batter that give it away.

Some players have the habit of immediately turning their attention away from the coach or changing their facial expressions after they see the sign indicating a play is on. The players or coaches observing the hitter and the runner will watch for the precise moment either of these players gives any indication a play sign has been given.

Which player, runner or batter, is to be watched depends on the game situation. If the situation calls for a potential running play — steal, hit-and-run, etc. — the spy assigned to watch the runner will be glued to the runner at first base. On the other hand, his eyes will be on the hitter in a sacrifice bunt or squeeze play situation.

Stealing signs is an iffy business, but the ballclub that can commit a little larceny in a clutch situation may pull out a victory. Doing this a few times over the course of a season adds measurably to a team's success in the pennant chase.

4
On the
Mound

Baseball is the only game where the ball is in the hands of the defensive team the majority of the time. The players who handle the ball the most are the pitcher and catcher which says something about the importance of this pair which is called the battery.

Without a good pitching staff, any baseball club would be hard-pressed to win a pennant. Good hitting might keep a club in the pennant race for a portion of the season, but when the hot days of late summer arrive, pitching depth becomes the key element for aspiring pennant contenders.

History has proven this time and time again. Over a 162-game schedule, a team blessed with good hitting can't overcome ineffective pitching. But good pitching can carry a mediocre hitting club in the pennant chase. With strong starting pitchers and sound relief, a team has a chance to be in every game. And a team that stays close has an opportunity to win.

HOW DOES A PITCHER ESTABLISH A STRATEGY?

Pitching strategy begins with knowledge of the hitters. All pitchers on each team keep a book on every hitter in their league. The book is the sum of everything a club knows about each hitter:

- His favorite pitch to hit
- The type of hitter he is (pull, straight-away, opposite-field)
- The location where he is most vulnerable (high, low, inside, outside)
- The type of pitch he handles least effectively (fastball, breaking ball, off-speed, etc.)
- Whether or not he likes to bunt for base hits
- His running speed
- How he reacts after a tight inside pitch (can he be rattled)

Each pitcher uses this information to establish, in light of his own physical and mental skills, a strategy for each hitter in opposing line-ups.

WHAT IS THE BIGGEST HAZARD IN CARRYING OUT A PITCHING STRATEGY?

The biggest hazard in carrying out a pitching strategy is consistently being behind the hitters on the ball and strike count, or as it is more popularly stated, "being in the hole." A .250 lifetime hitter becomes a .350 hitter when the pitcher is in the hole. Just as conclusively, a .300 lifetime hitter becomes a .250 hitter when the pitcher has him in the hole.

When the pitcher is in the hole, the batter can look for or sit on a certain pitch. That's why more home runs are hit when the ball-strike count is 2-and-0 or 3-and-1 than on any other counts.

Since the pitcher's main concern when he is in the hole is to get the pitch in the strike zone, he can't afford to be too "fine" with the pitch and go for the corners. What he has to do is give in a bit to the hitter and come more into the strike zone with the pitch.

It's worth noting that one change in recent years in pitching is the use of more breaking balls and off-speed pitches when the pitcher is in the hole. This gives the hitter more to look for — he can't sit back and wait on a fastball — but it can work to the pitchers detriment if the pitch isn't in the strike zone. When that happens, the hole gets deeper.

WHAT DOES THE STATEMENT
"THE PITCHER HAS 'GOOD STUFF'" MEAN?

When a pitcher's fastball is "live" with excellent movement, his breaking pitches break sharply, his change-of-pace or off-speed pitches have batters off balance, and his control is superb, a pitcher has "good stuff." When he has all of this going for him, he's hard to beat.

But in reality, pitchers seldom have all their good stuff game-after-game. More often, a pitcher may have a good fastball and breaking pitch, but ineffective control one game then the opposite the next game. On another occasion, he may have to depend on his off-speed pitches to get batters out because he lacks a live fastball.

There are numerous factors in a pitcher's ability to possess good stuff from one pitching appearance to the next. For one, he may experience more soreness or tenderness in his arm than normal, which affects his ability to feel loose when throwing his fastball. Consequently, he may have to go more to his breaking and off-speed stuff.

Another important element is fatigue from the last game. If a pitcher has thrown a lot of pitches in his previous assignment, he may not have enough time to regain his strength and stamina before his next outing. In this case, he may have to rely more on pitching savvy and pinpoint control to get the job done.

At other times, a pitcher may be too strong. This can occur when he has too much rest between pitching assignments because of days off or games rained out. Generally, when he is too strong, his pitches are alive, but he struggles with his control — usually early in the game. What separates the good pitcher from the mediocre is the ability to adjust. Even when he doesn't have his good stuff, the good pitcher adjusts his pattern to maximize his efforts with the pitches that are working for him that game.

HOW DOES A PITCHER "SET UP" A HITTER?

The real contest between the pitcher and the hitter comes down to whether the hitter gets a good pitch that he can really drive or ends up having to hit the pitcher's pitch which usually is in a location outside of the batter's hitting zone. The pitcher wants to put the batter in a position where he has little choice but to swing in a passive rather than an aggressive way.

It's important to understand that the pitcher's main objective in most situations is to keep the hitter off stride and not go for strikeouts. To meet his objective, the pitcher will move the ball around — making his pitches high or low, inside or outside — the strike zone to get ahead in the count. When he needs a pitch to get a tough out in a close game, the pitcher can go the location where the hitter is most vulnerable. He has the batter set up for his "out" pitch.

During this process, the pitcher may "show" a pitch to a hitter's strength to set up his out pitch to the hitter's weakness. It works this way: while pitching to a good high fastball hitter, the pitcher might throw a high fastball out of the strike zone, hoping the batter will go for it. This pitch is most effective when the pitcher is ahead in the count. Even if the hitter is proficient at hitting high fastballs, he's not likely to get "good wood" on that pitch. If the hitter lays off the high pitch, he may be nicely set up for a low curveball or slider to his weakest hitting area.

The key in setting up a hitter is for the pitcher to get ahead in the count. The effective pitcher will try to get ahead with one of the two pitches he can best control. The pitch he chooses will be thrown to a location across home plate and low in the strike zone. If the pitch results in a strike, the pitcher will start moving the ball around by throwing a variety of pitches. He is not likely to throw the same pitch in the same location. Setting up hitters is one the most intriguing aspects in baseball. Studying the pitcher's pattern adds enjoyment to watching a game on television.

WHAT HAPPENS WHEN THE PITCHER "PITCHES AROUND THE HITTER?"

Certain situations in a game dictate a pitcher not give a tough hitter anything good to hit. The most obvious is a tie game or when the pitcher's club is behind by a run with a runner on second base, two outs and a good hitter at bat.

In this situation, the manager may choose to have his pitcher pitch to the hitter instead of issuing an intentional walk, but he doesn't want his pitcher to serve up a fat pitch down the middle of the plate, either. What the manager will do is instruct his pitcher to "pitch around the hitter."

The hitter won't see anything good to hit. The pitcher will nibble at the corners either down-and-away or up-and-in with his fastball and keep the breaking ball low and out of the strike zone hoping the batter will swing at a pitch out of the strike zone and hit a weak ground ball or soft pop-up to a fielder. If that happens, the pitcher's club has retired the side without suffering any damage. If the batter lays off the pitches outside the strike zone, he receives an "unintentional walk" and is awarded first base. The pitcher will then pitch to the next batter who he feels he has a better chance of retiring.

WHY IS A 2-AND-2 COUNT WITH TWO OUTS AND RUNNERS IN SCORING POSITION CALLED THE "PITCH OF DECISION?"

If the count goes full — three balls and two strikes — the old merry-go-round will start. All runners will leave their bases as the pitcher makes his delivery. With that extra jump, the chances of a runner on first scoring on an extra-base hit are increased.

With less than two outs, the opposing manager is more likely to try a hit-and-run play on a 3-and-2 count than he is with a 2-and-2 count. This is another strong reason the pitcher tries to stay away from a full count.

The decision on the 2-and-2 count is crucial in keeping the pitcher out of potentially dangerous situations. On the 2-and-2 pitch in a critical situation, the pitcher is throwing the pitch he has the best control of in that particular game. The intense thought that goes into the selection of the 2-2 pitch truly makes it the pitch of decision.

WHAT IS MEANT BY THE STATEMENT, "PITCHERS GET AHEAD OF HITTERS WITH STRIKES AND GET THEM OUT WITH BALLS?"

One of the fun parts of baseball is watching how a good pitcher works the hitters. His first pitch is somewhere down in the strike zone with a primary objective getting the hitter to swing for an easy out. A secondary objective is to make that first pitch a strike — whether it's a called strike, swinging strike or foul ball.

If that first pitch is a strike (or even the second pitch), the pitcher expands his "pitching zone" — the area where he feels he can best retire a particular hitter — to include some areas outside of the strike zone. Subsequent pitches will intentionally be out of the strike zone in hopes the batter will swing. The pitching pattern continues in this manner as long as the pitcher remains ahead in the count.

Pitchers with a reputation for "being around the plate" normally are the ones who benefit when hitters chase pitches out of the strike zone. They get a lot of batters out on balls wide of the plate and also get the benefit of the doubt from the umpires on close pitches. There is no question about it, working with an expanded strike zone adds up to pitchers putting more W's in the win column.

WHAT IS THE BASIS OF THE OLD ADAGE, "MORE BASES ARE STOLEN OFF THE PITCHER THAN THE CATCHER?"

No matter how strong a catcher's throwing arm is, if a pitcher allows runners to get good jumps, it's virtually impossible for a catcher to throw out runners who have any kind of speed.

The base runner at first gets a good jump for two reasons:

1) The pitcher fails to keep the runner close to the bag.

2) He takes too much time in releasing the ball to the plate.

The biggest culprit in failing to keep the runner close is the absence of a good pick off move to first base. Without a good move to first, the runner is able to get a quicker start to second base. There is little concern of being picked off, so he gets a good lead and leans toward second, ready to take off as soon as the pitcher moves toward home.

Some pitchers have the fundamental flaw of using an exaggerated leg lift in their delivery from the stretch position. Instead of just striding forward and delivering the pitch, they make a high kick and then stride forward to deliver the ball. The extra time used for the kick allows the runner to get a good jump and beat the catcher's throw to second base.

In defense of the pitchers who use a high kick, they feel the only way they can get their best stuff is to lift the leg for maximum leverage and momentum. The pitcher with a slow delivery has to work exceptionally hard to perfect his pick-off move. Otherwise, any runner with fairly good speed is a threat to steal.

The pitcher with a good pick-off move to first and a quick delivery gives his catcher a better chance on almost every steal attempt. It's extremely difficult for a catcher to throw out a would-be base stealer if a pitcher is deficient in either of these areas — especially if he has a slow delivery.

Here is a time breakdown on a thwarted steal attempt:

1) **0:00.5** — Pitcher begins his delivery from the stretch position.
2) **0:01.3** — Maximum time pitcher should take to deliver the pitch to home plate.
3) **0.01.6** — Catcher receives the ball, shifts his feet and gets into a position to throw to second.
4) **0.03.3** — Catcher makes an accurate throw low and just to the right-field side of the base for the tag.

Any deviation in time from these numbers will generally result in a successful steal attempt. The key to preventing a steal is holding the runner close to the bag. If the pitcher can't do that, the odds of stealing the base increase.

INTENTIONALLY SCUFFING A BASEBALL IS ILLEGAL, BUT IT SUPPOSEDLY IS COMMONLY DONE. HOW DO PITCHERS "SCUFF THE BALL?"

Intentionally scuffing a baseball is definitely illegal, but in the modern trickery of pitching it's frequently employed. A scuffed ball is one where the cover is either scuffed by an abrasive material or cut with a sharp object.

Scuffing the ball creates greater air resistance on the side that has been tampered with. This disrupts the ball's smooth rotation when thrown hard, causing a more pronounced break in its direction than it would normally take. The exaggerated movement of the pitch is a distinct advantage for the pitcher.

Methods used in scuffing defy imagination. While few pitchers admit the practice, there are plenty who know how it's done. Among the methods:

- An abrasive, such as a small fingernail file hidden in the pitcher's glove can create a rough spot on the ball's cover.
- A sharpened belt buckle can be used to nick the ball.
- A small thumb tack pushed up through the leather in the heavily padded area around the base of the glove can cut the stitches in the ball or create a small nick in the cover of the ball.
- Long fingernails are an organic way for a pitcher to cut or nick the ball.

Now you know why the umpire always looks at the ball after it has been fouled off or bounces in the dirt. Without a doubt, a scuffed ball gives a pitcher a real, but unfair advantage.

The scuff rule was inserted in the rule book in 1982 to curb the use of balls with scuff marks on them. A pitcher guilty of delivering a scuffed ball after receiving a first-time warning is ejected and suspended for 10 days.

WHAT DOES IT MEAN WHEN IT IS SAID THAT THE PITCHER HAS "GOOD LOCATION?"

Location is a pitcher's directional control. It's his ability to throw the ball close to a specific area or target. There are several advantages for a pitcher who consistently has good location.

- He makes fewer pitches, which normally permits him to pitch more innings.
- He makes fewer fat pitches because he is rarely behind in the count.
- He gets the benefit of the doubt from the home plate umpire on close pitches.
- Base runners take fewer liberties.
- The fielders behind him do a better job of staying on their toes, ready for the ball to be hit to them.

WHAT IS THE DIFFERENCE BETWEEN A "TWO-SEAM" FASTBALL AND A "FOUR-SEAM" FASTBALL?

A good fastball is a combination of good mechanics, rhythm, control, velocity and ball movement. Pitchers at the big-league level have demonstrated ability in all these areas.

The one factor that rarely receives attention from the media is the movement of the fastball. Regardless of how hard a pitcher throws, if he hopes to consistently get batters out his pitches must change trajectory as they approach the plate.

The ball movement is created by the pitcher's grip, point of delivery, how the ball is released and the velocity of the pitch. To illustrate, look at two different kinds of movement on fastballs: *rising and running.*

A *rising fastball* tends to "ride up" from south to north as it approaches the hitter. To throw a rising fastball, the pitcher will grip the ball across the seams at its widest point. This grip gives the pitcher what is known as a "four-seam rotation" when the ball is released off the tips of the index and middle fingers with an overhand delivery (or what is commonly referred to as an 11 o'clock delivery for a right-handed pitcher — think of the position of the arm on a clock).

This sends all four seams on the ball spinning the same direction as they cut through the air. The cutting action of the raised seams, plus the velocity and backspin of the pitch cause it to rise.

By contrast, the *running fastball* moves east-to-west (from a right-handed pitcher to a left-handed hitter). It's held where the seams are at their narrowest and delivered from a 10 o'clock position.

The biggest difference in the pitches is what occurs at the point of release. The running fastball is more off the outside of the middle finger and rotates with a corkscrew effect, with the four seams rotating in more of an east-west fashion. This creates a sideways movement of the ball.

Another variation of the running fastball is the "sinking" fastball which moves both sideways and down. Batters tend to hit it on the ground making sinkerball pitchers very effective when a team needs a double play.

Movement on the fastball is so important because it affects the batter's swing. The hitter has to react and adjust his swing to compensate for the ball's movement with a corresponding effect on rhythm and timing — two important factors in hitting.

The diagram below demonstrates the difference in these two grips.

Rotation of Four-Seam Fastball

Rotation of Two-Seam Fastball

HOW DOES A SPLIT-FINGER FASTBALL DIFFER FROM A REGULAR FASTBALL?

There are two significant differences: the grip and the release. The index and middle fingers are close together on top and the thumb underneath on a regular fastball. As the name implies, the index and middle fingers are spread wide apart but basically remain on top on the split-finger fastball. The thumb is held to the side.

The difference in release comes in the backward rotation on the regular fastball, while the split-finger fastball squirts forward off the fingers with a forward rotation and makes a sudden dip as it enters the hitting zone. It's this quick downward movement that makes the split-finger fastball so effective.

This illustration shows the grip for the normal fastball (two-seam) and the split-finger fastball.

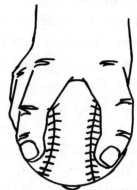

Normal Grip

Split-Finger Grip

HOW IS A CURVEBALL THROWN?

A curveball takes different arm, wrist and finger action than the fastball, as well as an adjustment in the pitcher's stride. Some pitchers shorten their stride about 3-6 inches for the curve, enabling them to get on "top of the ball." A hard snap of the wrist gives the ball better spin — and spin is the key to throwing a good curveball.

The arm action is basically the same as on the fastball until the arm is at the top of the delivery. From this point, as the arm continues forward, the wrist begins to turn over and snap downward.

Instead of releasing the ball off the fingertips as in a fastball delivery, the curve rolls over the index finger. Greater pressure is applied by the pitcher's middle finger, which helps pull the ball downward as the arm makes a sweeping motion down and across the body.

The best curveballs break down and away. On this pitch the hitter must adjust the height of his swing and carefully judge the pitch's speed.

WHAT CAUSES A CURVEBALL TO BREAK?

It's a law of physics that the faster air travels over a surface, the less pressure it exerts over that surface. The curveball breaks because it has a lot of topspin and the air flowing around the bottom of the ball travels faster than around the top. This means the air pressure is lower on the bottom of the ball than on top, causing the ball to break as it travels through the air.

Knowingly or unknowingly, pitchers utilize this principle of physics by trying to get the same four-seam rotation on the curveball as they do on the fastball (except the rotation is downward rather than upward or sideways). The four-seam rotation enhances the flow of air around the bottom of the ball as the wind resistance pulls on the raised four seams of the ball (see the diagram on the next page).

It takes a lot of practice and concentration to find the right grip and angle of delivery to release the ball so that the the rotation of the four seams maximizes air resistance. One thing is certain, the closer the pitcher comes to a four-seam rotation on the curve, the more topspin he'll get. The key to a good curveball is the tight spin caused by the four-seam rotation, and it's this tight spin that results in a bigger and sharper break in the ball's trajectory.

This diagram demonstrates the spin on a curveball.

Curveball Spin

WHAT'S THE DIFFERENCE
BETWEEN A CURVEBALL AND SLIDER?

Both are "breaking pitches," but the slider breaks more quickly and sharply than the curveball, and the break is less broad. The slider is also thrown harder. A good slider "slides" laterally about 6 inches and slightly downward. When a right-handed pitcher pitches to a right-handed hitter, it moves away rom the batter.

To throw the slider, the ball is held slightly off center with the fingers on the outside part of the ball. The release is similar to throwing a football — the wrist is stiff and the pitcher cuts across the ball with an inward turn of the wrist. The release is controlled by the index finger which applies more pressure than the middle finger, the opposite of the pressure point for the curveball. The difference in grips is shown below.

Curveball Grip

Slider Grip

WHAT PURPOSE DO CHANGE-OF-PACE PITCHES HAVE? WHAT ARE THE COMMON CHANGE-OF-PACE OR CHANGE-UP PITCHES?

The change-of-pace, change-up or off-speed pitch is essential to the success of today's pitchers because timing is a such a crucial factor in hitting. A batter's timing and reflexes are conditioned to the fastball, and the primary purpose of the change-of-pace pitch is to throw that timing off. By getting the batter out on his front foot, the change-up takes away his strength since all his weight is forward. In effect, the only power he can generate is with his arms because his body has been immobilized.

There are numerous change-of-pace pitches: the straight change-up thrown off the fastball, the screwball, the slip pitch and probably the two most used change-ups, the palmball and the circle change.

The key to the effectiveness of any change-of-pace pitch is to make it look as much like another pitch as possible. Most change-of-pace pitches are a variation of a fastball, but are thrown at about two-thirds the speed.

Most change-of-pace pitches are effective tools when the pitcher falls behind in the ball-strike count. They are effective pitches against home run-type hitters on any ball-strike count because the long-ball hitters tend to "sit on" the fastball, but they normally aren't good to use against weak or "contact-type" hitters with two strikes on them. In that situation, the contact hitter shortens up a bit on his swing and is not as easily fooled by the speed of the pitch.

Here is a look at the more prominent change-ups.

- *CIRCLE CHANGE* — thrown by forming a circle with the thumb and index finger with a regular fastball delivery. Because it's held off center, it tends to move down and away from a left-handed pitcher to a right-handed batter or vice versa. (See diagram on next page.)
- *PALMBALL* — thrown by securing the ball deep in the palm of the hand with all fingers slightly curved around it. There is very little finger pressure. Using a fastball motion, a good palmball has an exaggerated dip as it approaches the hitting zone. (See diagram on next page.)
- *SCREWBALL* — thrown by rotating the hand and wrist inward, causing the ball to be released between the ring and middle

fingers. This change-of-pace breaking pitch comes with its own aura of mysticism. It breaks the opposite way from the curve or slider. For example, a left-hander's screwball will break down and away from a right-handed hitter, while his curveball or slider will break into the right-handed batter. The thumb plays a key role by helping to increase the spin with a quick inward flip as the ball is released.

- ***KNUCKLEBALL*** — usually thrown by digging the fingertips, not the knuckles as the name implies, of the index and middle fingers into the seams of the ball. This is not necessarily a change-of-pace pitch, but it's definitely off-speed and the only exception to the rule that a pitcher must have several pitches in his arsenal to be a big winner. A good knuckleball pitcher can win with this one pitch. Its effectiveness is its unpredictability. Since there is little or no spin on the ball, it comes toward the plate with a "floating" or "butterfly" action, causing it to jump or swerve in either direction as it enters the hitting zone.

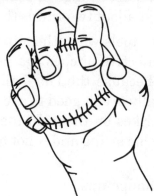

Circle Change Grip

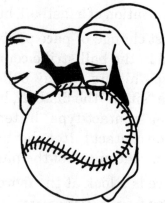

Knuckleball Grip

WHY IS IT IMPORTANT FOR PITCHERS TO KEEP PITCHES LOW IN THE STRIKE ZONE?

Pitching low in the strike zone is essential in the success of many pitchers. The ball that is up in the strike zone is easier for the hitter to see. He can see all of the ball when it is up in the strike zone, but only sees the top half when it is down in the strike zone. The high pitch also enables the batter to make a more level swing. The hitter doesn't have to drop the head of the bat to hit a pitch in the area of his hands because he can keep the bat almost level. A pitcher who keeps the pitch down and puts something on it will have an advantage.

5
Behind
the Plate

Catching has been called the toughest position to play for many reasons, not the least of which is the equipment the catcher wears. Many years ago, a catcher's gear was called the "tools of ignorance." The thinking was anyone who would wear all that heavy, sweaty gear must be crazy. While the equipment alone makes catching tough enough, in reality there is much more.

The catcher squats under a guy swinging a heavy bat and has to keep his eye on the ball as batter after batter waves his club through the air. He is in and out of this squat position more than a 100 times a game, constantly throwing his body in front of errant pitches to keep runners from advancing a base, taking foul tips off his body and blocking the path of runners trying to score.

But wait, there is still more.

The "more" in this case is the mental side of catching. A good catcher has to be smart and keep a "mental book" on every opposing batter so that he knows each player's strengths and weaknesses. He must also be aware of his pitchers' strengths and weaknesses so he can be in sync with each of them. Since the catcher is the only defensive player facing the field, he constantly reminds his teammates of game situations and possibilities, making him the defensive leader.

Because of this combination of physical and mental demands, catching is arguably the toughest position in baseball to play. Ballclubs play with more confidence when they have a catcher who knows his stuff.

WHAT GAME SITUATIONS PROVE A CATCHER, MORE THAN ANY OTHER PLAYER, MUST HAVE HIS HEAD IN THE GAME?

• With a left-handed hitter at the plate, the catcher will remind the pitcher to break toward first base on all ground balls hit toward the first base side of the infield. If the first baseman fields the ball, the pitcher will continue on to first base to receive a throw from the first baseman. The catcher's visual reminder to the pitcher to break toward first is to point his finger in that direction.

• With the bases loaded and less than two outs, the catcher will instruct the pitcher to throw the ball back to him on a ground ball back to the mound to force the runner coming from third base. The catcher will in turn throw the ball to first base to complete the pitcher-to-home-to-first double play. The visual reminder in this situation is the catcher pointing a finger at the pitcher and then at himself.

• On a sacrifice bunt attempt, the catcher in most cases will let the fielder making the play know where to make the throw. He will yell for the fielder to either throw to second or third base in order to retire the base runner, or take the sure out at first base. Because the play is in front of him, the catcher is in the best position to make this determination — he has a full view of the play.

• With an important runner on second base late in a close game, the catcher will step in front of the plate and flap both arms up and down. This is the catcher's reminder to the infielders to make every effort to knock the ball down on a ground ball hit into a hole between the infielders and headed for the outfield. Even if the batter-runner reaches first base safely, knocking the ball down and keeping it in the infield prevents the runner on second from scoring and gives the defense another chance to retire the side without the run scoring.

WHY DOES THE CATCHER POSITION HIMSELF SO CLOSELY TO THE BATTER?

The catcher squats as close as possible to the plate without interfering with the batter's swing for several reasons:

- The closer the catcher is to home plate, the easier it is to handle low pitches.
- It puts him closer to the strike zone, enabling the umpire to get a better look at low pitches.
- It puts him in a better position to throw on stolen base attempts.
- He's quicker in moving out to field bunts and slow rollers in front of home plate.

Catcher's good positioning...
close to the hitter and giving a good target

WHAT IS THE CATCHER'S TOUGHEST PLAY?

The play at home plate where ball and base runner arrive almost simultaneously is probably the most difficult play a catcher has to make. Unlike at second and third bases where the approaching runner must stay on the bag once he reaches it, a runner coming home need only touch the plate as he goes by. This allows the runner to generate more momentum as he approaches home than at any other base.

To combat this, the catcher will attempt to block the plate and catch the ball at the same time the runner arrives. He blocks the plate by placing his left foot on the third base corner of home plate. Then, as he catches the throw, the catcher drops to his left knee to put a shin guard between the runner and home, keeping the runner from reaching the plate. The catcher in this situation has the protective equipment to help him avoid injury.

Technically speaking, if the catcher blocks the plate before the ball arrives, he could be guilty of **OBSTRUCTION**. But this is rarely called because of the bang-bang nature of the play.

Catcher's toughest play

DOES THE PITCHER OR CATCHER DECIDE
WHICH PITCH IS TO BE THROWN?

The catcher will usually give the pitcher a signal for what pitch he thinks is best in a situation. But today, more and more managers or pitching coaches signal the catcher for the type of pitch the manager wants. The final responsibility for what pitch is thrown, however, normally rests with the pitcher.

The reason for this is when there is an element of doubt in the pitcher's mind about the pitch the catcher wants, his concentration will be divided. It's tough enough to get hitters out when the pitcher agrees with the catcher or manager, much less when he has doubts.

So when the pitcher disagrees with the pitch selection, he will (or should) shake the catcher off and have the catcher signal for the pitch he wants to throw. In the final analysis, it's the pitcher who gives up a home run in a crucial situation — not the catcher or manager.

WHAT DOES IT MEAN WHEN IT IS SAID THAT "SOME HITTERS GUESS AGAINST THE CATCHER INSTEAD OF THE PITCHER?"

In the chapter on hitting, we discussed how hitters "sit on a pitch" or "look" for a certain pitch to be thrown in a certain location. Normally, a hitter will concentrate on "guessing" with the pitcher in these situations.

Some catchers, however, tend to fall into a pattern — just like pitchers do — when signaling the type of pitch they want. Regardless of who is pitching, catchers become predictable in the type of pitch they call in certain ball-strike counts in certain game situations. Aware of this, hitters "guess" with the catcher on what type of pitch will be thrown.

Let's look at an example: with runners in scoring position, a predictable catcher might consistently call for a breaking pitch on a 2-and-2 count. On the other hand, with the bases empty and the count 2-and-2, he might regularly signal for a fastball.

Most teams keep tabs to see if a catcher has a consistent pattern in certain situations. If he does, you can easily understand why many hitters tend to guess against the catcher rather than the pitcher.

SHOULD A CATCHER CONSIDER A BATTER'S WEAKNESSES OR A PITCHER'S STRENGTHS WHEN CALLING FOR A PITCH?

That's an easy one — the pitcher's strengths. The ideal situation is a pitcher on the mound with the kind of stuff — fastball, curve, slider, change-up, etc. — and the location on these pitches, to set up each hitter for a pitch to his most vulnerable area.

This kind of pitcher is rare, however, so what most catchers have to work with are pitchers whose strengths are to the weak points of some hitters and to the strong points of others. This causes the catcher to work different pitchers in different ways, and the same pitcher in different ways. As the game progresses, the catcher is going to have his pitcher mix up his pitches and the location of these pitches.

But when it comes down to needing an "out" pitch in a clutch situation, the catcher will call for the pitcher's best pitch on that day in the best location. If that happens to be in the batter's groove, so be it.

For instance, a low fastball pitcher is pitching to a good low fastball hitter, who is known to be weak on breaking balls such as curves and sliders on the outside part of the plate. The catcher knows this, but he also knows his pitcher is noted for occasionally throwing a "hanging breaking ball," which is a hitter's delight.

Just because a hitter has problems with breaking balls doesn't mean the catcher should signal for a steady diet of them. The pitcher may be better off just showing the breaking ball to the hitter, hoping the batter will chase a bad pitch.

But when a strike is needed in a clutch situation, the catcher will call for a fastball and put his target at the batter's knees. Then it's a case of strength against strength and becomes simply a matter of whether the pitcher is better at pitching low balls than the batter is at hitting them.

YOU HEAR A LOT ABOUT THE IMPORTANCE OF THE PITCHER THROWING TO A "GOOD TARGET." WHAT IS A GOOD TARGET?

A target is the spot the catcher wants the pitch to be thrown. To ensure that his target is a good one, the catcher will use his mitt and body.

The ease, confidence and timing the catcher gives a full body target can have an almost hypnotic effect on the pitcher. The pitcher responds to this "alive" target with increased concentration — which is the purpose of the target in the first place.

An alive target finds the catcher moving his body over slightly — either to the inside or outside parts of the plate — when the catcher wants the pitch thrown in either of those directions. This keeps the catcher's mitt in the middle of the his body, presenting a more precise target than the one where the catcher merely extends his mitt into the area desired. Most catchers will wait until the pitcher begins his windup before moving and putting the mitt up to give the target to prevent the hitter from taking a quick look back to see where the catcher has positioned himself.

Catcher's good target

WHAT IS A PITCHOUT? WHY DOES A CATCHER CALL FOR IT?

A pitchout is a pitch thrown deliberately out of the strike zone where the batter can't hit it. This allows the catcher a quick and unobstructed shot at thwarting a steal attempt, attempting to pick a runner off one of the bases, or breaking up a hit-and-run or suicide play. Sometimes it's even used to determine if a hitter is going to attempt a sacrifice bunt or hit away. Normally, a hitter will give away his intentions as the pitch approaches the plate.

In most cases, the pitchout call is made by the manager instead of the catcher. Regardless of who makes the call, the odds of retiring a runner must be weighed against the prospect of putting the pitcher in the hole on the ball-strike count when using a pitchout. To keep the pitcher out of a situation where he gets behind in the count, many managers only signal for a pitchout when the pitcher is ahead in the count.

The game situation usually is the most important factor in the pitchout decision. But a pitcher's control, as well as the relative ability of the base runner and batter, also factor into the decision.

WHAT IS THE "INFIELD DRIFT" A CATCHER HAS TO CONTEND WITH WHEN CATCHING A POP-UP?

On pop-ups behind home plate, the rotation or "drift" of the ball is back toward the playing field. To compensate for this infield drift, the catcher attempts to catch pop-ups with his back to the infield. In this position, the ball is coming back toward him and makes an easier play.

Once the catcher locates the ball, he tosses his mask in the opposite direction so that he doesn't trip over it as the ball "drifts" back toward the infield. The higher the pop-up, the more drift it takes.

IT HAS BEEN SAID THAT A CATCHER CAN HURT HIS TEAM IN THE WAY HE RETURNS THE BALL TO HIS PITCHER. WHAT DOES THIS MEAN?

A little-publicized attribute of a catcher is the way he returns the ball to the pitcher. A good return throw is about chest high on the pitcher's glove side. Return throws that are all over the place — up and down, here and there — cause the pitcher to use too much energy and effort. They also affect his ability to concentrate. Bad throws simply divert his attention away from the job at hand and a terrible throw that gets away from the pitcher may allow base runners to advance.

6
In the
Field

Over the course of a 162-game schedule, the worst teams win at least 54 games and the best lose at least 54 games. What happens in the other 54 games separates the winners from the losers. The difference comes down to a team's ability to play sound, fundamental baseball. Nowhere is this more important than in the field.

A bit of wisdom passed down through the years says, "Give 'em only three outs, make 'em earn their runs, and you'll have a chance to win." Without quality pitching and consistent defense, it's tough for a club to win a pennant — regardless of offensive prowess.

Playing defense is more than pitching, fielding, throwing and catching. It involves knowing the hitters' strengths and weaknesses, proper placement in the field, anticipating where the ball will be hit and having a keen sense of the base runners. As you will see in this section, effective defensive play is as much mental as physical.

HOW IMPORTANT IS THE KNOWLEDGE OF THE HITTERS IN WHERE THE INFIELDERS POSITION THEMSELVES?

Good infielders play the percentages in their defensive positioning. Through observation and concentration, they gain a keen sense of playing hitters where they are most likely to hit the ball.

They know whether a batter normally pulls the ball, hits it straight-away or is an opposite field hitter. They are also aware of how he hits against certain pitchers, as well as how and where he hits certain pitches. Furthermore, they know the running speed of the hitters, and whether they like to try to bunt occasionally for a base hit.

Even if an infielder has lost a step or two over his playing career, he can make up for it with his "mental notebook" on the hitters. This is the reason an older, more experienced infielder who declares free agency prefers to sign with a club in a familiar league. In a strange league, he no longer has this advantage, and he knows he can't be as good defensively.

WHAT HELPS AN INFIELDER
GET A "GOOD JUMP" ON THE BALL?

Knowledge of the hitters is a prominent factor in the ability to get a "good jump." But the little extra that helps the shortstop and second baseman anticipate plays is knowledge of the pitch to be thrown and the pitcher throwing it.

Since both middle infielders (second baseman and shortstop) can see the catcher's signals to the pitcher, they often anticipate where the ball will be hit. Given the type of pitch, the expected location of the pitch and the pitcher's velocity, they will lean or shift slightly with the pitch — being careful not to shift too soon and tip off the batter. For example, an exaggerated shift by the shortstop to his right would be a tip-off for an off-speed (change-up) pitch.

Let's look at what might go through the mind of the shortstop: "Curveball is called. The pitcher likes to keep it away from this particular hitter, so the batter will probably be out in front and pull it toward the hole. I will lean a little to my right."

WHY IS IT SAID THAT "THE SHORTSTOP IS THE KEY
TO A TEAM'S INNER DEFENSE?"

For two very basic reasons:

1) He has a lot of ground to cover.
2) He gets more fielding opportunities than the other infielders.

Without quality play at shortstop, a club's defense will always come up short.

There are several things that you can watch that make the shortstop position somewhat different from that of the other infielders:

- A shortstop's stance may be a little different; he may point his toes out instead of straight ahead enabling him to move quickly to either his right or left with a small jab step.

- Knowledge of hitters and the type of pitcher on the mound are probably more important to the shortstop than any other infielder. Because he has so much ground to cover, knowledge and experience enable the shortstop to anticipate plays and vary the ways he plays the hitters. Even though he varies his positioning only slightly, it could mean the difference between a solid base hit and a possible inning-ending double play.

- The shortstop will lean forward as the pitch reaches the plate. By placing his body in motion, he is better able to overcome the body's inertia and move more quickly to the ball.

- Along with the second baseman, the shortstop prefers to use a small, flat glove with minimum of padding. This type of glove keeps the ball from getting buried deep in the glove's pocket, allowing a quicker throw to a base.

GAME-IN AND GAME-OUT, WHAT IS THE TOUGHEST DEFENSIVE PLAY IN BASEBALL?

Experts generally agree that the toughest play is the ball hit deep into the hole between the shortstop and the third baseman. On this play the shortstop must range far and deep to his right onto the edge of the outfield grass, field the ball and, in one fluid motion, throw the runner out at first base.

What makes this play so difficult is that the shortstop must be quick enough to get to the ball and then reach across his body to make a backhanded play. Since he is going away from first base, he has to plant his back foot and make a strong throw back across his body. No easy task.

Unfortunately, few fans really appreciate the difficulty of this play. The great shortstops make it appear easy. The good shortstops may get to the ball, but lack the strong arm necessary to throw the runner out. Others simply watch the ball sail past them into left field for a hit.

The shortstop who game after game can make that play adds immeasurably to the his club's success over the course of a season. It's the reason a shortstop who hits .250 but executes this play with precision commands a multimillion dollar salary — and the fans' applause.

The ground ball deep "in the hole" on his backhand side is the shortstop's toughest play.

WHAT IS A PIVOT? WHY IS IT IMPORTANT TO A CLUB'S INNER DEFENSE?

It is said that a pitcher's best friend is the shortstop-to-second baseman-to-first baseman double play. The key element in this double play is the pivot by the second baseman. For example, with a runner on first base and less than two outs, the shortstop fields a ground ball and tosses the ball to the second baseman to force the runner out at second. The second baseman then pivots and relays the ball to the first baseman to complete the double play.

It is called a pivot because the second baseman receives the throw from another fielder while he is looking and moving away from first base. In a split second, the second baseman must try to catch the ball, tag the bag, or pivot toward first base, and fire the ball to the first baseman.

Quickness in completing the pivot is essential. With the runner barreling down on him, the second baseman must execute the play and then leap to avoid the sliding runner. Second basemen capable of executing this play with precision come at a premium. In the illustration below, you see the second baseman as he executes the pivot.

The second baseman executing a pivot.

WHY IS THIRD BASE CALLED THE "HOT CORNER?"

Third base is called the "hot corner" because there are more right-handed hitters, which increases the frequency of hard-hit balls in the direction of the third baseman. A batted ball also gets to the third baseman more quickly than it does the other infield positions since the third baseman plays closer to the hitter than the other infielders.

There are several things to observe as you watch the third baseman play the hot corner.

• He generally uses a bigger glove than the ones used by the shortstop and second baseman. This provides him with vital extra inches in spearing batted balls on his backhand side and in diving after balls in the hole to his left. He also carries his glove closer to the ground than the other fielders so he can already be down on the ball if it is rocketed on the ground in his direction.

• It is important that the third baseman try to reach everything in the hole to his left, since he is moving toward first base while the shortstop is moving away from it. The third baseman also has a shorter throw. Because the third baseman needs to be in a position to cut off the ball hit to his left, he will play as close to the hitter as his courage, quickness and sure hands allow. He has less ground to cover in this position, but he is also more vulnerable to the hard-hit ball.

• The third baseman moves around and varies his position more than any other infielder. With fewer than two strikes, he may be even with the baseline or up in front of the base to defend against a possible bunt attempt. He may also move a step either way from pitch to pitch, anticipating where he thinks the ball might be hit.

By the way, the term "hot corner" originated with a Cincinnati sportswriter in the late 1800s. After observing a game where the third baseman was almost decapitated by a couple of line drives, he wrote of the third base position as the hot corner!

One of the most important things an infielder learns is when not to throw the ball. For example, after catching a short fly ball with a runner on base or after receiving a relay throw from the outfield, an infielder will "run the ball in" if there is no play. But he will be ready to make a throw.

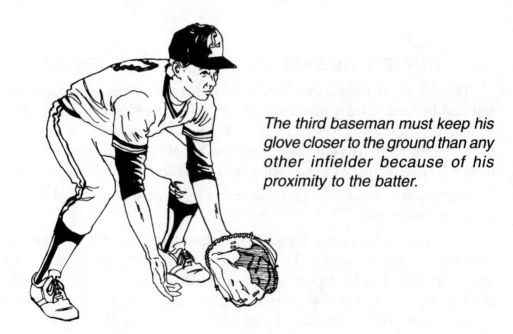

The third baseman must keep his glove closer to the ground than any other infielder because of his proximity to the batter.

WHY ARE THERE NO LEFT-HANDED INFIELDERS OTHER THAN THE FIRST BASEMAN?

The reason is quite simple: the left-handers' natural throwing motion at the other three infield positions is away from first base. In order to make a throw to first, the left-hander has to field the ball, pivot his entire body and then step to get the throw off. On the other hand, the right-handed infielder simply takes a single step to make his throw. His body momentum is already moving in the direction of first base.

Arguably, the easiest position of the other three — shortstop, second base and third base — that a left-hander could play is third base. He can handle balls hit up the line better than a right-hander, but the grounder in the hole between the third baseman and the shortstop is tougher to handle since it is on his backhand side.

Playing second base is virtually out of the question for a left-hander. Imagine how he would have to make the pivot on a double play — once he receives the ball, he has to tag the bag, step back, and then spin around toward the outfield before making the throw to first base. It would take a really slow batter/runner for a southpaw to execute a double play.

WHAT ADJUSTMENTS TAKE PLACE WHEN THE SHORTSTOP AND SECOND BASEMAN PLAY AT "DOUBLE-PLAY DEPTH" RATHER THAN AT "NORMAL DEPTH?"

When there is no runner on first base, the shortstop and second baseman will play at normal depth. In this alignment, the shortstop and second baseman will play as close to the batter as possible while being as far away from the batter as possible. What this bit of double-talk means is that they will play as deep as they can and still be in a position to retire a batter-runner going to first base.

This may put the infielder a step or two closer to home plate than where he would play with a slower runner at bat. This variance in positioning is why we often see close plays at first base even against the slower batter-runner.

Whenever a runner is on first with fewer than two outs, the shortstop and second baseman will play at double-play depth. As a general rule, this brings the shortstop and second baseman in four or five steps toward home and one or two steps closer to second.

On a ground ball, this alignment enables them to get to the base in time to take a throw, retire the runner and throw to first to get the double play. This will vary, however, to account for the type and speed of the hitter.

The shortstop will play as far away from second base as possible with a strong right-handed pull hitter at the plate and a runner on first who is not particularly fast. He won't play so far away, however, that he can't get to the base in time to make the play if the ball is hit on the right side of the infield. The second baseman will do the same with a left-handed hitter who pulls the ball.

WHY AND WHEN IS THE "INFIELD IN" DEFENSIVE ALIGNMENT DEPLOYED?

With an important run on third base for the opposition and less than two outs, the manager will have the infielders play in. In this alignment, which is called "infield in," all infielders move in about three or four steps inside the base lines.

The purpose is to keep the runner on third from attempting to score on a ground ball. It will deter the runner from advancing on third if the ball is hit directly at an infielder. But this alignment has an obvious weakness — the infielders simply can't cover much ground because of their proximity to the batter. As a consequence, it's difficult to make a play on a sharply hit ball not hit directly at one of the infielders.

The manager may use the "infield in" alignment at any point during a close game. Against a particularly tough opposing pitcher, he may deploy it early in a game, thinking his team may not score many runs and they must do everything possible to hold the opposition to as few runs as possible. Normally in the early innings with a runner on third and less than two outs, managers prefer to play the infield back and give up a possible run in order to prevent the offensive team from having a big inning.

WITH A RUNNER ON FIRST BASE, WHY DO BOTH THE SECOND BASEMAN AND SHORTSTOP MOVE INTO THE OUTFIELD ON A BALL HIT BETWEEN THE OUTFIELDERS?

On an extra-base hit between the outfielders, the second baseman and shortstop will move into the outfield for the relay. For example, on a ball hit into the alley between the left fielder and center fielder, the shortstop is the lead man. The second baseman is the trail man, positioned about 30 feet behind the shortstop.

Once the outfielder playing the ball retrieves it, his throw should be about chest high to the lead man who takes it and relays it to the appropriate base or "cutoff man." In this case, the third baseman is the cutoff man. The first baseman is the cutoff man on an extra base hit into the right-center field alley.

The second baseman, or trail man, is there for two very important reasons:

1) In case the throw from the outfielder sails over the lead man's head.

2) To shout instructions to the lead man as to what play should be made once he receives a throw from the outfielder — home, third base, run it in (here the lead man would turn and run the ball back to the infield).

A similar lineup on an extra-base hit into the alley in right-center field will find the second baseman as the lead man and the shortstop as the trail man.

IN A CRUCIAL LATE-INNING SITUATION, THE DEFENSE WILL PUT THE BUNT PLAY OR WHEEL PLAY ON. WHAT HAPPENS ON THIS DEFENSIVE MANEUVER?

The score is tied 2-2. There are runners on first and second with no one out. A relatively weak hitter is at bat. It appears to be a certain bunt situation. In this situation, the defensive club's manager may well use the bunt play, or as some refer to it, the wheel play. On this defensive play, the third baseman will ignore third and charge the plate to cover the left side of the bunting area. The first baseman will charge in and cover the right side, while the pitcher will protect the area in front of the mound. The second baseman will cover first base, while the shortstop will move over to cover third.

The key to the success of this play lies with the shortstop. If he breaks too soon for third, he gives the play away and the runner on second can easily get a better jump toward third base. To make the play work correctly, the shortstop will move in close behind the runner, showing a possible pick-off play. At the same time, the pitcher will look back toward the runner. Once the runner freezes, the pitcher will turn and deliver the ball to the plate and the shortstop will break to cover third base.

To combat this defensive maneuver, the offense will sometimes attempt to steal third. As the shortstop breaks toward third, the runner will also break. The batter fakes a bunt to draw the third baseman in. Then it simply becomes a foot race between the shortstop and the runner for third. To counter, the defense will have the shortstop make a false break toward third to get the runner leaning toward that base. Then the second baseman will break toward second base for an attempted pick-off play.

The defensive team will only use the bunt play when it is fairly certain the batter will be bunting. Otherwise, it leaves some very big holes for the batter.

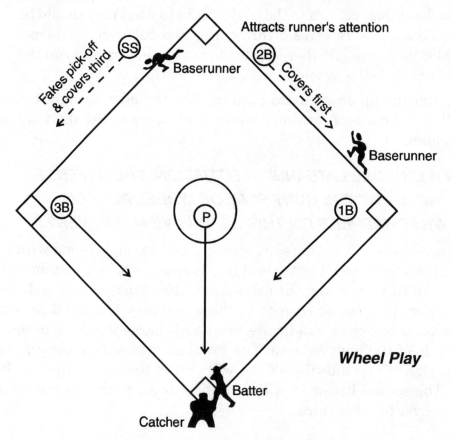

Wheel Play

WHY DOES THE TEAM THAT IS AHEAD
"GUARD THE LINE" LATE IN THE GAME?

In the latter stages of a close game in which the defensive leads or the score is tied, the manager will probably have the first and third basemen guard the base lines. This helps prevent ground balls from getting past them and down the lines for extra-base hits.

A ball hit into the hole between infielders is only a single. A ball hit down the line is usually a sure double. A single means the offensive club still needs to advance the runner another base to put him in scoring position.

What the defensive manager is doing in this situation is playing the percentages. He would rather force the offensive team to get two singles in the hole rather than a possible double down a base line.

WHY DOESN'T THE FIRST BASEMAN HOLD THE RUNNER ON
WHEN BOTH FIRST AND SECOND BASE ARE OCCUPIED?

With a runner in front of him, the runner on first base really has nowhere to go. Therefore, unless a bunt situation is in order, the first baseman plays behind the runner to provide better field coverage.

That doesn't mean that he completely ignores the runner. In fact, with less than two outs, he is going to play reasonably close behind the runner until the pitch is made. This prevents the base runner from getting a big lead and lessens his chance of breaking up a double play on a grounder.

WHAT ADVANTAGE DOES A LEFT-HANDED FIRST BASEMAN
HAVE OVER A RIGHT-HANDER?

All other things being equal (fielding ability, quickness, agility, etc.), the left-handed first baseman has several natural advantages over his right-handed counterpart. To begin with the lefty has an advantage on the double play and bunt play. He can field the ball and throw naturally to second or third since his momentum and arm motion are in that direction. The right-hander has to field the ball and turn his body to make the throw.

The left-hander also has a natural advantage on pick-off attempts because his glove hand is on the inside part of the bag. This makes it easier for him to catch the throw and put the tag on the runner in one motion. The right-hander, on the other hand, has to bring his glove across his body to make the tag.

A final advantage for the southpaw first baseman is that his glove hand is on the side where there is more fair territory. This gives the defense better protection in the hole between first and second.

WHAT DETERMINES THE OUTFIELDERS' POSITIONING?

Where the outfielders position themselves for each batter depends on the type of hitter, the pitcher, the score, the number of outs, the speed of the base runner(s), and the count on the batter. Outfielders often adjust their positioning slightly from one ball-strike count to another.

For example, with a 1-0, 2-1, or 0-1 ball-strike count, the outfielders generally play at normal depth from home plate. If the count goes to 2-0 or 3-1, they may play a little deeper and move slightly toward the side of the field of the hitter's position in the batter's box. With two strikes on the hitter, the outfielders may come in a little bit. The reasoning behind this is hitters normally will shorten up on their swing with two strikes.

WHAT IS AN OUTFIELDER'S TOUGHEST PLAY?

The toughest play for an outfielder is the line drive hit directly at him. The difficult aspect of this play is that the outfielder doesn't know how fast the ball is coming to him or whether it is a sinking line drive or a rising line drive.

Another tough play for the right fielder and left fielder is the batted ball that has either a hook or slice in it. A ball hit by a right-handed hitter down the left field line will hook toward the foul line. A ball hit by the same hitter down the right field line will slice toward the right field foul line. The reverse is true for a ball hit by a left-handed batter. Accordingly, the left fielder and the right fielder have to adjust defensively as they move to catch the ball.

A line drive hit directly over his head is an outfielder's most difficult play.

WHY IS IT IMPORTANT FOR AN OUTFIELDER TO "RUN AN INFIELDER OFF" ON A POP FLY?

On a pop fly ball where both an infielder and an outfielder can make a play, it's the outfielder's responsibility to make the play by "running the infielder off" and making the catch. The outfielder makes the play since he is moving into the ball and the play is in front of him. Conversely, the infielder on this play is moving backward away from the infield.

It's also worth noting that the center fielder is the prime defender. In this role, he always takes preference over the infielders and other outfielders on any fly ball he can reach.

HOW DOES ARTIFICIAL SURFACE AFFECT DEFENSIVE PLAY?

On artificial surfaces, all outfielders generally have to play deeper to cut off a hit into the alleys (area between the outfielders), since the ball travels much faster on the artificial turf. They also must be more cautious as they advance on a hit that lands directly in front of them. The ball bounces much higher on the artificial surface. If an outfielder is too aggressive, the ball may easily bounce over his head for an extra-base hit.

Infield play is also affected. On the positive side, infielders get truer bounces and fewer bad hops. On the negative side, the hardness of the surface causes the ball to reach the infielders much more quickly. As a result, infielders must play deeper or closer to the area where the infield and outfield meet, which makes their throws longer. To retire a runner going to first base, they have to get rid of the ball faster, increasing the chances of a poor throw.

WHY ISN'T A THROW ON THE FLY BY AN OUTFIELDER TO HOME OR ANOTHER BASE CONSIDERED A GOOD PLAY?

An outfielder's throw must be low enough to allow the infielder who is the cutoff man a chance to cut the ball off and prevent base runners from advancing an extra base. That's the reason a throw all the way home on the fly is not normally a good throw. It looks good from the stands and brings a chorus of "oohs" and "ahs," but it's not an intelligent play with more than one runner on base.

The reasoning is simple: if the throw goes over the head of the defensive player at the base, the chances of the runners advancing to another base are increased. Hitting the "cutoff" man stationed 40-45 feet in front of the base prevents an "overthrow" and offers the defense numerous options, depending upon the game situation.

7
Managerial
Strategy

There is no real fan who has never said, "If I were manager, I know what I would have done in that situation." Just about everyone who passes through the ballpark turnstiles is a manager at heart.

It doesn't matter what brings on this thinking. Fans who are really into the game have a pretty good idea not only of what they would have done, but who they would have done it with. They can be quite vocal about it, too. "Why didn't you get that bum out of there before he gave up that home run, Mr. Manager?" is a chorus that rings through the stands after an opposing hitter belts one out of the park in a crucial situation.

One of the things that stands out about baseball managers is the instantaneous nature of most of his decisions, reacting to the game situation as it unfolds. It leaves him open to a lot of second guessing.

Now, most grandstand managers will give the first guess to the manager, but reserve the second guess for themselves. There's nothing wrong with that, is there? One of the fun parts of being a fan is helping the manager manage — even if it is after the fact!

In this chapter we will look at some of the thinking that goes into the manager's first guess. That should make it easier for grandstand managers to take the first guess more often — which is the same one taken by the manager.

WHY IS THE FIELD LEADER IN BASEBALL CALLED THE MANAGER, BUT IN OTHER SPORTS HE IS CALLED THE COACH?

Before 1900, the on-the-field leader of a baseball club was called the captain. He was usually one of the players who was given the added responsibility of making decisions while the game was being played. A non-player in charge of off-the-field activities was called the manager.

As captains begin to retire as active players, they didn't want to give up their duties in running the on-the-field activities. Many of them began handling both duties both on and off the field. The former captains gradually moved the non-players out of the managers' jobs and eventually began to place their own men into the on-the-field leader's role.

After the turn of the century, the term "manager" identified the person who ran the club on the field. The off-the-field manager became known as the general manager.

Other sports like football and basketball, did not develop in the same way baseball did. These sports were more popular at the college and scholastic levels where the role of a coach was more prominent in teaching how to effectively play the sport in question.

WHAT IS THE MANAGER'S TOUGHEST JOB?

The consensus among experts is that handling the pitching staff is the manager's most difficult responsibility. This includes selection of the staff, who to use in what role, and the daily decision of when to make pitching changes and who to use when that decision is made.

Working with his pitching coach, the manager will generally divide the pitching staff into two groups: starters and relievers. Today, most managers prefer a five-man starting rotation, which means each pitcher starts every fifth game. There are cases, however, when the fifth starter misses a regular turn because of off-days, rainouts, etc. When he is not scheduled to be in the regular rotation, the fifth starter will act as a long (several innings) reliever.

For some managers, selection of a starting rotation is easy. Unless injuries force changes, they can send the same five starters out week after week. Others managers, however, may have two or three capable starters, but struggle to find a fourth and fifth. To offset this, they may use the "committee system" and pick from a group of three or four candidates, depending on the opponent and ballpark among other variables.

Most managers carry either 10 or 11 pitchers. Those with a reasonably stable starting rotation will carry only 10, which allows them the luxury of having another everyday player on the roster. This can be crucial in pinch-hitting situations. Managers who have difficulty fielding a solid starting rotation must carry an extra pitcher or two.

Once a starting rotation is established, the relief corps is put into place. Relievers are divided into four categories: 1) long man, 2) middle man, 3) setup man and 4) short man or closer. Of these four, the short man or closer gets the most attention. A ballclub that lacks a strong closer who can come into a game in a tough situation and stop the other team is unlikely to contend for the pennant.

Each of the other relief pitchers also has a specific role. Earlier, it was noted that the fifth starter is sometimes used as a long reliever. The long reliever is generally used if the starting pitcher is "knocked out" of the game in any of the first three or four innings.

Most managers prefer to have a right-hander and left-hander ready to use as long relievers. If the opposing team, for example, has loaded its batting order with left-handed hitters against a right-handed pitcher, the manager will call on the left-handed long reliever if a change is needed.

The middle man is normally used from the fifth to the seventh innings. He might come into a game when his club is slightly ahead, slightly behind or the score is completely out of hand. Sometimes a middle man is used as a long reliever. This often occurs on a 10-man pitching staff or when the manager prefers to go with the right-left scenario discussed earlier. It's more likely to occur when a manager only has a limited number of right-handed or left-handed relievers.

The setup man sets the stage for the closer, usually working the seventh and eighth innings. Managers want both a left-hander and right-hander for this role, and it's not uncommon to see both in the same inning when trying to protect a lead.

The closer is the money pitcher. His job is to come in with his team ahead and close out the win. He is rarely used in any other situation, although he may come in when a game is tied, but that also is rare. The closer can be either left- or right-handed. But in either case, he has to throw strikes and consistently get batters out.

WHAT FACTORS HELP A MANAGER DECIDE
WHEN TO CHANGE PITCHERS?

Sometimes the decision to make a pitching change is easy for the manager. At other times, however, what seems the thing to do from a fan's viewpoint may not look the same from the manager's angle.

Fans are concerned about the game being played today. The manager has to look ahead. He may have to endure some rough spots — and a sprinkling of boos with a starting pitcher because he has an overworked relief corps, an important series with a tough club coming up or a couple of doubleheaders over the next few days.

At times, the manager's decision to stay with a starting pitcher longer than usual is based on his knowledge of the pitcher. Some veteran pitchers have a history of starting slowly, especially when they have had too many or too few days of rest between starting assignments.

Under normal conditions, however, a manager will make a change after the starter has given up several runs or doesn't appear to have his good stuff. In an attempt to keep the other team from scoring any more runs, he will bring in a long reliever and give his club a chance to battle back into contention.

The decision to replace a starting pitcher in the early or middle innings is usually minor compared to the one the manager must make with a one- or two-run lead late in the game. Several things go through a manager's mind in situation. Fatigue is the first thing he looks for. It's usually the reason a pitcher loses his good stuff — the movement of his fastball and the location of his pitches. When a pitcher gets tired, managers know the fastball and positive attitude are soon to follow.

There are numerous signs that a pitcher is tired. The manager and his pitching coach will look for such indicators as:

- The way the ball comes off the bat in fair territory. Line drives, long fly balls and hard-hit grounders, even if they result in putouts, will have the manager warming up a relief pitcher.

- The location of the pitches is a clue to the manager and coach that a pitcher is running out of gas, even if he is not giving up many hits. They will pay special attention if the pitcher starts to miss the catcher's target and consistently falls behind in the ball-strike count.

- The dugout observers also pay attention to the number of pitches a starting pitcher has made during the game. Prior knowledge gives them a good idea how many pitches he can make before he begins to tire. Once the pitching count reaches this number, the manager will have his bullpen throwing at the first sign of trouble for the starting pitcher.

- To a lesser degree, these signs also could be tip-offs that a pitcher is tiring:
    a) constantly going to the rosin bag.
    b) excessive manicuring of the pitching mound.
    c) taking longer between pitches.
    d) making unnecessary pickoff throws to first base.

The manager doesn't always wait for a pitcher to show obvious signs of fatigue before making a change. He may decide before an inning starts to take the pitcher out if an important run gets into scoring position with the opponents' better hitters due to come to bat.

Then again, he might decide in advance to let the pitcher stay in the game until the winning run comes to the plate — then make a change if the tying run comes to bat. Or he may make a prior decision to remove the pitcher if he walks a batter with less than two outs.

This is just a sampling of the more technical side of a pitching change. Because of the importance of pitching, the manager thinks ahead about relief pitching strategy more than he does about any other maneuver.

WHEN THE MANAGER OR PITCHING COACH GOES TO THE MOUND TO CONFER WITH THE PITCHER, WHAT DO THEY TALK ABOUT?

Most mound conferences are held to settle down a pitcher who is having control problems or is being hit hard by opposing batters. An encouraging word, a tip on technique or strategy, a little chewing out, or an amusing statement may be intermixed by the manager or coach as the situation dictates. Once in a crucial game situation, my manager strolled to the mound and said with a straight face, "Lefty, let's get these guys out — the beer's getting hot!"

Sometimes the visit is meant to buy a little time to give a relief pitcher a chance to warm up properly. Other times, especially in crucial situations, the manager may want to be certain the pitcher understands how to pitch to a certain hitter. The manager or his pitching coach will go to the mound to avoid any misunderstanding.

The manager or coach has to make the most of each mound visit, because only one visit per inning is permitted. On the second visit in an inning, the pitcher must be replaced.

The common practice is for the pitching coach to make the first visit to the mound to confer with the pitcher. The manager generally makes the second trip in an inning if it's necessary to remove the pitcher from the game.

SINCE THE PITCHER BATS IN THE NATIONAL LEAGUE, HOW IS RELIEF PITCHING STRATEGY AFFECTED?

Because the National League does not have a designated hitter rule, pitchers take a regular turn at bat. This means National League managers have to make decisions that their American League counterparts don't have to worry about.

It's not uncommon, for example, for National League managers to find themselves in this situation: top of the eighth inning, the opposing club has rallied to tie the score at 3-3 and there are first and third base with two outs. A right-handed batter is due to face a tiring right-handed pitcher.

In the American League, the manager would bring in a relief pitcher and hope he gets the final out of the inning. He would keep him in the game in hopes of holding the opponent at bay to give his team a chance to score a go-ahead run in the bottom of the eighth or ninth innings.

It's not that simple for the National League manager. A complicated factor in his decision is the fact that the pitcher is scheduled to hit third when his club comes to bat. Add to this equation an overworked relief staff and the manager really has a tough decision. If he brings in a relief pitcher to get the final out, he faces the prospect of having to use a pinch hitter in the bottom of the eighth inning and another relief pitcher in the top of the ninth inning. Should the game go into extra innings, the manager may find himself short of available relief pitchers.

The National League manager is faced with three questions:

1) Should he use a reliever at this point to get the final out?

2) Should he leave the pitcher in the game to try to retire the side without any more runs scoring?

3) Should he substitute two players — a relief pitcher and a fielder — and insert the fielder in the ninth slot in the batting order?

The latter decision is one that National League managers often make. It offers the manager a viable alternative to using a relief pitcher for only one out. By inserting another player in the lineup at the same time he changes pitchers, the manager can strategically adjust his batting order so the relief pitcher can remain in the game after his club takes its turn at bat.

When two players are substituted at the same time, the rules allow a manager the option of where to place the two players in the batting order. Subsequently, he places the fielder in the ninth slot and the pitcher in the batting spot of the fielder removed from the game. Normally this will be the last player to hit in the previous inning.

As you can see, relief pitching strategy for a National League manager can be more complex and much more involved than that of the American League manager. Since the pitcher takes a turn at bat, the National League manager has to deploy more relief pitchers as well as use more pinch hitters.

WHAT ARE SOME PRINCIPLES A MANAGER CONSIDERS WHEN MAKING OUT A BATTING ORDER?

One of the most important jobs of the manager is to construct the batting order. Most of the time he follows certain principles to select an effective order. They are:

- The better hitters will be near the top of the batting order where they will have the most opportunities to bat.

- Hitters who are best at getting on base will bat before the heart of the batting order (the third, fourth and fifth hitters).

- The batting sequence will be placed as strategically as possible to combine the runs batted in (RBI) potential and the running speed of the hitter.

How a manager utilizes these basic principles depends mainly on the personnel he has available. The job is easier for managers who have more talent to work with. They are able to use the same batting order game after game. Blessed with good personnel, their most unusual act is to occasionally switch a couple of players around in the batting order, or send up a pinch hitter once in awhile to bat for a starting player.

Other managers adhere to these principles by using different players at different times in different batting positions. Because of injuries, lack of ability or managerial preference, players are platooned almost on a daily basis. This means two players "share" a position. The decision as to which one plays depends on the opponent, the stadium and, to a great extent, the opposing pitcher (right- or left-handed).

Generally, if a manager platoons at a position, he will have both a right-handed and a left-handed hitter available. If a right-handed pitcher is on the mound, the left-handed hitter plays. With a lefty on the hill, the right-handed hitter will play.

Some managers have a knack for devising a batting order which hides a club's weaknesses and maximizes its strengths. They seem to have a feel for the right time to play certain players and when to keep them out of the lineup. They have a sixth sense for putting the right man in the right batting slot. As a result, they get better production than each individual player's statistics indicate they should.

WHAT DOES A MANAGER USUALLY LOOK FOR WHEN FILLING THE NINE POSITIONS IN THE BATTING ORDER?

Leadoff Hitter

Most of the time, managers want a hitter who has proven his ability to get on base to be the leadoff hitter. For a leadoff man to be effective, his on-base average should be around .400. This means for every 10 times he goes to bat, he should be getting on base in any fashion an average of four times. That should put the leadoff hitter on base 250-275 times a season. A good eye at the plate, an ability to bunt for base hits and exceptional speed are assets a good leadoff man will have.

Second-Place Hitter

In the second batting position, managers prefer an above-average hitter who can consistently put the ball in play. Patience is also a sound attribute. If the leadoff hitter is a base stealing threat, the No. 2 batter must have the patience to give the runner a chance to steal.

The advantage the second-place hitter has with a speedy runner on first base is that he sees more fastballs. Most catchers call for more fastballs with a runner at first because it's easier to throw out would-be base stealers. By seeing more fastballs, the second hitter should be able to put the ball in play more readily and place it behind the runner into right field if a hit-and-run play is on.

Many managers prefer a left-handed hitter in the second slot because he can better protect the runner on first. It's more difficult for the catcher to see the runner at first base with a left-hander at the plate and a left-handed hitter can pull the ball into the big hole between first and second base.

Third-Place Hitter

This is the slot where managers prefer to put their best all-around hitter. While it would be a plus if he were capable of hitting 20-25 home runs a year, it's more important that he move the runners around to score. The third-place hitter has to be a good RBI man.

If there is a choice between two hitters for the third and fourth spots, and if one is left-handed and the other right-handed, the left-hander will probably hit third. There are two reasons for this thinking:

1) With two men on base, he has a bigger hole between first and second at which to aim.

2) He will normally hit into fewer double plays.

The double play threat is a prominent consideration in who hits third. Since nothing kills a rally more quickly than a double play, there is a strong preference to put a faster man in the third slot, regardless of the side of the plate he hits.

Fourth- and Fifth-Place Hitters

The fourth and fifth places in the batting order are where the power hitters take their turns at bat. Who hits cleanup (fourth) and who hits fifth are basically determined by which side of the plate they hit from and the type of pitcher. If a manager is fortunate enough to have both a left- and right-handed long ball hitter, he will probably place the right-hander in the fourth slot, especially if the third place hitter is a left-hander. The left-handed hitter then will hit fifth. If the manager hits the two left-handed hitters back to back, he leaves himself vulnerable to the opposition bringing in a left-handed relief pitcher in the late innings of a close game. As a general rule, left-handed hitters experience more difficulty hitting left-handed pitchers because they don't face as many left-handers as right-handers. With only one real long ball threat, the decision of who hits fourth is relatively easy. This is the position where the long ball hitter will take his cuts. The manager will then probably use a batter with some speed and hits well with runners on base for the fifth slot.

Sixth-Place Hitter

The sixth hitter probably varies more than any position in the batting order. On a club with several power hitters, one usually will be sixth in the batting order.

On the other hand, if a club relies on speed, the sixth position is like a second leadoff hitter. It's a place for a contact hitter with good speed. A stolen base in this part of the batting order makes sense with mostly singles-type hitters to follow.

Seventh-Place Hitter

The seventh slot is where the manager who relies more on speed and baserunning strategy will place a hitter with decent bat control and the ability to hit behind the runner.

On a power-laden club, this position is where managers tend to place a slumping power hitter. Moving a hitter down in the lineup takes pressure off so he can concentrate on just meeting the ball.

Eighth- and Ninth-Place Hitters

The type of hitters who fill these slots in the order depends on the league. In the National League, where the pitcher hits ninth, managers prefer a little speed in the eighth position. When the eighth-place hitter gets on base and the pitcher is called on to sacrifice, the pitcher has a better chance for success if the runner has some speed.

In the American League, where pitchers don't bat, the worst hitter seems to be slotted in the eighth position. American League managers lean toward a better-than-average hitter in the ninth place in the batting order. They prefer to head into the top of the order with a runner on base at least 30 percent of the time.

WHAT IS THE STRATEGY BEHIND THE HIT-AND-RUN? WHEN IS IT BEST USED?

The increased emphasis on aggressive running play has made the hit-and-run more prominent in the offensive arsenals of many managers. The hit-and-run helps keep the defense off-balance. It keeps the fielders moving and that creates more holes. It also helps keep teams out of double play situations.

The manager's decision to use a hit-and-run play is determined by many things:

- Score
- Number of outs
- Skills of the base runner
- Ball-strike count
- Inning
- Placement of the runners
- The hitter
- The pitcher

Typically, the hit-and-run play is used with a good contact batter at the plate and a runner on base who may not necessarily be a base stealing threat. The batter is expected to swing at the pitch regardless of whether it's in the strike zone or not in order to protect the runner who is moving toward second.

Rarely will a manager use the hit-and-run play with a home-run hitter at the plate. The hit-and-run places the batter in the position of having to swing at the pitch regardless of its location, and the manager ordinarily prefers to let the home-run hitter swing at a pitch to his liking. In baseball "slanguage," the manager doesn't want to take "the bat out of the batter's hands" by putting him into a must-swing situation.

The situation where the hit-and-run is most commonly used occurs when the ball-strike count is 3-and-2, 3-and-1 or 2-and-0. In these situations the pitcher will be concentrating harder on throwing strikes, giving the batter a better chance to get a good pitch to hit.

The ideal time to attempt the hit-and-run with almost any hitter in the batting order is on a count of 3-1 or 3-2. In either case, he doesn't have to swing at the pitch if it's out of the strike zone because it will be ball four.

The number of outs and placement of the runner (or runners) also enter the hit-and-run equation. With two outs and a runner at first, the hit-and-run is seldom a wise strategy. With the hitter required to swing at the pitch, it lessens considerably his chances of hitting the ball solidly for an extra-base hit. Even if the batter singles and advances the runner to third, another base hit is still needed to score the run. The odds favor giving the hitter a chance to select a good pitch and trying to go for an extra-base hit.

Another situation where the hit-and-run is rarely used, even though on the surface it might appear to be sound strategy, is with the tying run on third base and the go-ahead run at first late in the game with no one out and a 3-and-2 count on the hitter. The reason the hit-and-run is not good strategy here is that if the batter strikes out and the runner breaking from first is thrown out at second, there are then two outs and the tying run is still at third. If the next hitter is put out, a prime scoring opportunity has been lost.

The possibility of a strikeout, throw-out play usually overrides any advantage the manager might have in sending the runner on the pitch. The type of hitter and the speed of the runner at first are strong considerations in what the manager decides, but even if the batter in this situation hits into a double play, the runner from third base will still score the tying run. That is the manager's first concern: getting the tying run home.

Properly executed, the hit-and-run is a great play. It gets the fielders moving around, puts runners in scoring position and leads to scoring runs — which enhances the chances for more victories.

WHAT IS BEHIND THE MANAGER'S DECISION
ON WHO TO USE AS A PINCH HITTER?

A manager always thinks several hitters ahead. Consequently, he may already have decided on the use of a pinch hitter before the need arises. But what batter should he use?

Which pinch hitter to use depends on whether the opposing pitcher is right- or left-handed, the score of the game, number of outs, the inning and game situation. Of these, game situation probably carries the most weight in the decision-making process.

On average, a big-league club has six or seven potential pinch hitters when the game begins. As pinch-hitting opportunities develop, a manager will use the pinch hitter best suited for the situation. For example, a singles-type hitter may be used if the situation calls for someone to just get on base. If an important run is on third base with less than two outs, a pinch hitter who is known to hit fly balls might be used in hopes a fly ball will be hit deep far enough to allow the runner to tag up at third and run home.

A hitter with good bunting skills may be called to advance a runner a base, while still another may be used when an extra-base hit is needed. At other times the situation may call for a pinch hitter with the kind of speed that reduces the chance of hitting into a double play.

Another crucial factor in the manager's pinch-hitting decision is the pitcher the pinch hitter will face. Most managers prefer to go with a right-handed batter against a left-handed pitcher, or left against right, when the game is on the line. Also, the manager isn't likely to send a poor curveball hitter to face a good curveball pitcher, just as he prefers not to pinch hit a left-handed batter against a tough southpaw.

Some managers are fortunate enough to have a pinch hitter deluxe who is capable of hitting against right-handers and left-handers with equal effectiveness. Even if a manager has a top-notch pinch hitter available, he has to be careful in how he uses him. He wants to have him available for a tough, clutch situation late in a tight game. So, the manager is not going to use his best pinch hitter to lead off the seventh inning with his club behind by two runs. If he does, who is he going to use in the ninth inning with the winning run on base?

WHAT IS POSSIBLY THE MOST INTRIGUING LATE-INNING DEFENSIVE PREDICAMENT FOR A MANAGER?

Most baseball experts believe that a manager is faced with his toughest decision when his club is in the field with runners on second and third base, no one out and the manager's team leading by a one run in the bottom of the ninth inning. If the manager moves the infielders in from their regular playing positions to protect against the tying run scoring on a ground ball, the possibility of the winning run scoring from second base on a scratch hit increase. The manager could choose to walk the next hitter intentionally to set up a potential double play at any base, but the plot thickens if the player at bat is followed by one of the opposing team's better hitters.

When there is a big difference in the comparative abilities of the batter due to bat next and the batter in the on deck circle, the manager usually chooses to pitch to the weaker hitter with his infield playing back in their normal positions. If this hitter is retired without the runners advancing a base, the manager will choose to walk the next batter intentionally to set up a double play situation at any base.

It's important to note that the offensive team is more dangerous with runners on second and third base than with the bases loaded. Why? In a bases-loaded situation, any ground ball the pitcher or an infielder can handle is a potential home-to-first double play. That possibility doesn't exist with first base open and a grounder results in only one putout.

HOW DOES THE MANAGER DECIDE
WHEN TO PUT THE STEAL SIGN ON?

There is not much of a decision to be made when a manager has a premier base stealing threat. But in the absence of this kind of base runner, a manager has to make the decision of whom to run and when to run him.

Other than the runner's speed and baserunning prowess, a manager's biggest decision is the ball-strike count and expected pitch. Since breaking and off-speed pitches are the best to attempt a steal, the manager often tries to "guess" what type of pitch will be thrown.

For example, if the first two pitches are fastballs resulting in a 1-and-1 count, the manager may like the odds of the next pitch being something other than a fastball. Immediately, he flashes the steal sign.

Unless he has an exceptionally talented base stealer, a manager usually foregoes the steal with no one out. He doesn't want to kill a potentially big inning by having the inning's lead-off hitter thrown out trying to steal. The batters due to hit during the inning will be the ultimate factor in this decision.

Another situation where a stolen base is rarely attempted is in the ninth inning with less than two outs and the tying run on first base. Purists say it just isn't good baseball strategy to have the potential tying run thrown out attempting to steal in the ninth inning.

WHEN IS A SQUEEZE PLAY USED? WHAT'S THE DIFFERENCE
BETWEEN A "SUICIDE" AND A "SAFETY" SQUEEZE?

A squeeze play occurs when the batter attempts to bunt a runner home from third base. Situations that may call for a squeeze play include: one out with a weak hitter at the plate, a close game with a fairly good bunter and a pitcher with a slow windup.

There are two types of squeeze plays: the "suicide" squeeze and "safety" squeeze. The difference between the two is in the actions of the runner on third base.

On the suicide squeeze, the runner breaks for home just as the pitcher reaches the point of release of the pitch to the batter. In other words, the runner is on his way home at the same time as the pitch heads toward home (hence the term "suicide"). If the runner breaks too early, the pitcher will pick it up and simply pitch out to a left-handed hitter or make the pitch low and in to the right-handed hitter. Regardless of the side of the plate he hits from, the batter will be unable to effectively bunt the pitch, making the runner a sitting duck.

Another important point: when the sign is flashed to the hitter by the third base coach, the hitter must indicate with a sign of his own that he received it to insure that the runner doesn't run into a certain out. Nothing is worse than the batter missing the sign for a squeeze play with a key run on third base. If the batter doesn't attempt to bunt, the runner coming from third is a sure out.

On the safety squeeze, the runner doesn't break for the plate until he sees that the ball is bunted safely and he feels he can make it. For the safety squeeze to work, the runner at third must have above-average speed and not break to the plate too quickly. The batter's actions differ on each squeeze play, too. On the suicide squeeze his job is to bunt the ball on the ground regardless of where it is thrown. On the safety squeeze, the batter will bunt the ball only if it is a good pitch — and try to place it away from the pitcher. If successful, the runner from third should score easily.

THE HEAD GROUNDSKEEPER IS OFTEN CALLED A MANAGER'S "10TH MAN" ON THE FIELD. HOW DOES HE EARN THIS TITLE?

Most of us think of the groundskeeper as the individual who sees that the playing field is maintained with a manicurist's touch. He does that, but is not beyond tailoring the infield to fit the strengths and weaknesses of the home team, too. That's what earns him the title of the manager's "10th man."

There are several ways the groundskeeper assists the home club. The first that comes to mind is when a sinkerball pitcher is starting for the home club. In this situation, the area in front of home plate is excessively wet and covered over with dry dirt. Since there will be an unusual number of ground balls hit by the opposition, the wet turf slows the ball after its first bounce. This enables the infielders to reach balls that might otherwise go through the infield for base hits.

The base paths are another area that may be doctored in much the same way. With a club in town that likes to run and steal bases, the groundskeeper may soften the base paths by thoroughly wetting the first 20 feet or so and then covering with dry soil.

Another trick is to raise or lower the pitching mound in the bull-pen. The bullpen mound is supposed to be 10 inches high like the regular mound. Making it higher or lower tends to disturb a relief pitcher's rhythm when he takes to the regular pitching mound.

The infield grass is another favorite of the groundskeeper. In those big-league parks where the infield is still grass, the grass is cut according to the defensive ability of the home infielders. For instance, the height of the grass could vary from the left side of the diamond than to the right side. If the shortstop has good range and the second baseman doesn't, the grass on the left side could be normal, but higher than normal on the right side which would slow the ball down and give the second baseman a better chance to reach it.

Ability, range of the infielders and the type of hitters on the visiting club are also factors in how high or low the grass is cut.

The outfield grass is not left out by the groundskeeper, either. He varies the height of the grass according to the abilities of the various outfielders. For example, if the left fielder is relatively slow, the grass on his side of the field may be kept reasonably tall to keep the ball from going up the alley.

The baselines along the infield also may get into the act. The groundskeeper might lay the chalk a little higher if his club is good at laying down bunts for base hits. He might go so far as to slant the base paths in toward the playing field slightly, too.

When the opposing pitcher relies on breaking balls and off-speed pitches, the groundskeeper might lay out the batter's box 2 or 3 inches closer to the mound. This enables the batter to move up in the batter's box to hit the breaking stuff before it breaks. The smart groundskeeper varies his "tricks" to keep the opposition and umpires guessing. When he does, he's definitely an asset to the home club.

8
Off the Field

Baseball is no longer solely a game played on the field. Agents, attorneys, legal entanglements and strikes — all centered around financial considerations — have significantly changed the game.

Financial considerations stand front and center today. The box-car salaries and long-term contracts club owners threw around for years have pushed the game to the brink of financial disaster. Now, with owners wanting to pull in their horns by implementing a salary cap and players wanting to continue with business as usual, neither side is bent toward compromise.

What led to this owner versus player mentality was the *1976 BASIC AGREEMENT* which changed the owner/player relationship forever. Under terms of the agreement, the old *RESERVE CLAUSE* which bound a player to one club was replaced by the *REENTRY SYSTEM.* The whole idea behind the reentry system was to allow experienced players to play out their *OPTION* and offer their services to the highest bidder. As the saying goes, the rest is history.

It's easy to get confused when trying to understand terms associated with the reentry system. Add the owners salary cap plan to the equation and it tests the knowledge of even the most astute fan. Hopefully, what follows will bring clarity to some of the terms that relate to off-the-field activities.

HOW DOES THE FREE AGENCY SYSTEM WORK?

Players with six or more years experience in the big leagues and not tied to a long-term contract can file for free agency. Free agents may negotiate with any club for their services.

Most free agent players (mainly through an agent or attorney) receive bids from all interested clubs, including their former club. In most cases, the highest bid will entice a player to accept a contract. But the desire to play for a pennant contender or in a particular city or geographical location often plays a role in the final decision.

Under terms of the latest baseball agreement, a club losing a free agent receives an amateur draft choice as compensation.

AREN'T THERE SEVERAL POTENTIAL PROBLEMS INHERENT IN THE FREE AGENCY SYSTEM?

Critics of the system point to several potential problems. One is money. Some ballclubs have to yield by default. They are not in big TV markets and don't have the money to compete for the better free agents. Worst of all, they end up losing one or two quality players from their own club to other clubs because of their inability to compete financially. It seems some clubs are torn down as quickly as they are built up.

Another underlying problem may be the long-term contract. Will the player with a long-term deal and fat salary continue to care enough to do his best? Will he play when slightly injured? Will he give it his all when the chips are down? If he doesn't, what can management do about it? Release him and swallow a multimillion dollar contract? Trade him? Who would want the risk at that price? The jury is still out on this aspect of free agency.

Then there's always the risk of a player's career being cut short by a crippling injury. Pitchers are more susceptible to injury than other players, and for that reason, a long-term contract for a pitcher is probably the biggest gamble. Many clubs have already had to eat guaranteed long-term agreements because of a player's injury or poor performance.

WHAT ARE THE KEY PROCEEDINGS
IN A SALARY ARBITRATION HEARING?

When management and a player are locked in a salary impasse, a best bid is submitted by both parties to an impartial arbitrator. Both parties then appear before the arbitrator to present their case. The hearing is usually conducted in a hotel suite. The arbitrator, the player and his agent or attorney, and a representative of the player's team are present for the hearing. The arbitrator sits at one end of the bargaining table, with the respective parties to the arbitration facing each other on either side.

The player's position is presented first. His agent/attorney offers the player's outstanding skills and abilities to justify the salary figure requested. Then the club presents its case, stressing the negatives to back up the lower salary offer made to the player. After a brief recess, rebuttals are held.

Once the dispute goes to arbitration, there is no compromise. The arbitrator has to choose one salary recommendation over the other, usually giving his decision about 24 hours after the hearing. A player can file for arbitration after completing his second full year in the big leagues. He also has to be signed to play under a one-year contract.

CAN A FREE AGENT'S FORMER CLUB
OFFER HIM ARBITRATION?

A free agent's former club can offer arbitration. It must be done by the end of the first week in December. By offering the free agent arbitration, the former club retains its right to a compensatory draft pick if the free agent signs elsewhere.

A player offered arbitration has about two weeks to accept or reject the offer and another couple of weeks to negotiate with his former club. If he fails to re-sign with his former club by the first full weekend in January, he becomes ineligible to re-sign until May 1. A free agent player who isn't offered salary arbitration prior to the declaration date in early December cannot negotiate with his former club until May 1.

WHAT ARE SOME CRITERIA AN ARBITRATOR USES
TO MAKE HIS DECISION?

Criteria used by the arbitrator to make a decision between the player's salary request and that filed by the ballclub's management include:

- Length of playing time and consistency of his performance.
- Quality of performance during the past season.
- Past compensation and salaries of players with comparative performances.
- Performance of the club the player plays for.
- Past history of the player's injuries or any other physical or mental defects.
- His leadership abilities and public appeal.

PLAYERS FREQUENTLY MOVE UP AND DOWN
FROM THE MAJOR LEAGUES TO THE MINOR LEAGUES.
WHAT RULES GOVERN THIS MOVEMENT?

From the beginning of the season in April until Sept. 1, a major-league club has a 40-man roster, but may keep only 25 players on the **ACTIVE ROSTER.** After that date, the roster may grow to 40 players until the end of the season.

The 15 players not making the active roster are optioned to minor-league clubs. Unless a player is out of options, he can be brought back to the major-league (parent) club at any time.

A player is out of options when he has been called up to the parent club and sent down to the farm club in three previous years. Regardless of how many times he goes up and down in a season, it counts as only one option.

There are two situations, however, where a player can be sent down and recalled without counting as an option: if he goes to the farm club and is recalled within 20 days, and if he is called up after Sept. 1 when rosters can expand to 40 players.

HOW DOES THE WAIVER PROCESS WORK?

A waiver process is required to trade a player from midnight July 31 until the end of the regular season. The waiver process starts with a club putting a player on the waiver list (a club can place as many as seven players on the waiver list each day).

Every other club has as many as three business days to file a claim. If no claim has been filed at the end of the three business days, that player has cleared waivers and can be traded to another club at any time.

If the player is claimed, the club holding that player's contract has to make one of two decisions:

1) Allow the player to go to the club that put in the claim.

2) Withdraw the waiver request.

The club that controls the player and the claiming club have 48 hours to work out a trade. This window gives the controlling club a chance to test the trade market without having to give the player away. Players under the **Ten-and-Five Rule** (see page 99) have the right to veto the trade.

If there are multiple claims, priority is determined in reverse order of current league standings. Clubs in the league in which the player performs have first shot at him. If no one in that league puts in a claim, clubs in the other leagues have their turn.

HOW DOES THE MAJOR-LEAGUE AMATEUR DRAFT WORK?

The amateur draft was established in 1965 to equalize talent and hold down the escalation in bonus payments to untried players. (That reason has since gone by the boards in a big way.) The draft is held during the first week of June.

During the three-day draft, major-league clubs acquire negotiating rights to high school and eligible college players. Selections are made in inverse order of the previous year's standings, alternating by league. Currently, the worst National League club drafts first in even years, with the American League's worst team getting the honor in odd years.

To be eligible for the draft, a player must have completed his senior year of high school or junior year in a four-year college or university. A player attending a junior college can be drafted after his first or second year. The draft is applicable only to players from the United States and its territories, and Canada.

Under a policy established for the 1992 draft, a club retains rights to a drafted player for five years. The policy has been challenged by the Player's Association, which wants to reinstate the one-year rule for clubs retaining a player's draft rights.

WHAT IS THE RULE 5 DRAFT?

This is the draft by major-league clubs and their minor-league affiliates of current minor-league players of other clubs. There are three phases of the Rule 5 draft:

1) draft of all players by the major-league clubs not protected on another major-league club's 40 man roster

2) draft of AA players by AAA clubs

3) draft of A players by AA clubs

Some very stringent policies make drafting a player under Rule 5 a rare occurrence, especially at the big-league level. Prominent among these is the fact that the player drafted must remain with the club which claims him for the whole season or be offered to other clubs through waivers or to his former organization if he clears waivers.

If he is put on waivers and claimed by another club, the claiming club must keep him all year. If he clears waivers, he then must be offered to his original club. If that club passes, he can be farmed out by the team drafting him to a minor-league affiliate.

Each major-league club pays $50,000 for a player drafted to the major-league level. At the AAA level each pick costs the drafting club $12,000. At the A level it's $4,000 per pick. Clubs draft in inverse order to their finish the prior season, with each league alternating.

WHAT DOES THE ANNUAL MAJOR-LEAGUE CALENDAR LOOK LIKE?

- **First two weeks in January** — Salary arbitration filing period.

- **End of first full week in January** — Last day for clubs to negotiate with their players who have become free agents and have rejected arbitration.

- **Third week in January** — Salary arbitration figures exchanged between the club and the player (or agent).

- **First three weeks in February** — Salary arbitration hearings before the independent arbitrator.

- **Mid-February** — Players report voluntarily for spring training.

- **First of March** — Earliest mandatory day for players to report to spring training.

- **Second week of March** — Clubs can renew the contracts of players who have not signed new contracts.

- **March 29** — Last day clubs can ask waivers in order to a player without to pay his salary for the coming season.

- **First week of April** — Major-league season opens; rosters reduced to 25 players.

- **May 1** — Clubs may resume negotiations with their former players who became free agents.

- **May 15** — Players released following the end of the previous season may be re-signed by the club that released them.

- **First of June** — Annual amateur draft of high school and college players.

- **Mid-July** — All-Star Game.

- **July 31** — Last day to make inter-league trade without the player going through waivers.

- **First week of August** — Hall of Fame inductions.

- **August 31** — Last day a player can be placed on a major-league roster and be eligible for postseason play.

- **September 1** — Active rosters of major-league clubs can be expanded to 40 players.

- **First week in October** — American and National League Divisional layoffs begin.
- **Mid-October** — World Series.
- **Late October** — Free agent filing period begins at the conclusion of the World Series.
- **Mid-November** — Last day (TBA) when clubs can offer salary arbitration to eligible players.
- **First week in December** — Annual owners meeting and Rule 5 draft.
- **December 7** — Last day clubs can offer salary arbitration to their former players who became free agents.
- **December 19** — Last day for free agents offered arbitration to accept or reject offers.
- **December 20** — Last day for clubs to tender contracts for the coming season.

WHAT IS THE ALIGNMENT OF DIVISIONS IN EACH LEAGUE? HOW DOES IT AFFECT THE PLAYOFFS?

Under baseball's realignment in 1994, each division now has three divisions — East, Central and West. The new alignments in each league break down as follows:

NATIONAL LEAGUE

EAST	CENTRAL	WEST
Atlanta	Chicago	Colorado
Florida	Cincinnati	Los Angeles
Montreal	Houston	San Diego
New York	Pittsburgh	San Francisco
Philadelphia	St. Louis	

AMERICAN LEAGUE

EAST	CENTRAL	WEST
Baltimore	Cleveland	California
Boston	Chicago	Oakland
Detroit	Kansas City	Seattle
New York	Milwaukee	Texas
Toronto	Minnesota	

Each division winner and the non-divisional winner with the best won-loss record make the playoffs. The division winner with the best record plays the non-divisional winner in the first round, with the other two divisional winners playing each other. The first round is best of five games (the first to win three games wins).

The two winners will then play each other in a best-of-seven league championship series. The winners (first to win four games) play each other in the World Series, also a best-of-seven event.

WHERE WILL THE MONEY TO PAY ESCALATING SALARIES COME FROM?

You and I will pay for it, one way or the other. Some will come through higher ticket prices. But the real salvation for most baseball franchises will be pay-per-view TV. It may be the only means available to generate the revenue necessary to combat rising salaries and expenses.

Let's look at an economic example. In order to sign a free agent, a club digs into the coffers for an additional annual outlay of $5 million. To help pay the tab, the club raises ticket prices an average of $1 per seat. Suppose the addition of the player helps increase attendance by 100,000 next season. Along with this improvement in attendance comes an increase in concessions and parking that generates an additional $600,000 in gross revenue. The home club has to give about 25 percent to the visiting club which leaves $450,000. That will pay one-tenth of the salary of the $5-million player. It's obvious that big revenues have to be generated elsewhere to pay higher salaries.

Conventional TV network executives failed to offer a competitive bid, a good indication of where they think baseball revenues are headed. The replacement is a new baseball TV network, created especially for the purpose of holding TV revenues at or near previous levels. Obviously, this may be a reach. If a significant reduction in income is the outcome from the baseball network, pay TV may end up being the only way to create any substantial new earning power.

It appears that's what a lot of club owners are betting on. The Baseball Commissioner's office previously tried to limit the scope of baseball on the cable super stations. Legislation is needed for this action and has been discussed at various times in Congress.

What this means for fans is their favorite club may soon be on its own sports channel, available to us by subscription. This will produce mind-boggling figures for the number of games televised, but whether it will produce the income owners are hoping for remains to be seen.

The basis for this conjecture is that unless some form of revenue sharing is worked out, the rich may just get richer and the poor, poorer because most clubs will cater to a regional market. Teams in larger viewing areas will have more exposure. As a result, the question becomes, will baseball become a two-tier structure made up of the 'haves' and 'have-nots'?

WHAT ARE SOME TERMS AND PHRASES WHICH APPLY TO OFF-THE-FIELD ACTIVITIES?

Disabled List

Injured players are on this list for periods of 15, 21 or 60 days, depending on the severity of the injury. Placement on the list takes the player off the active roster allowing club management to add another player as a replacement. Only two players can occupy each disabled period at any other time.

Farm System

Each major-league club will have at least one farm club on each minor-league level — Class A, AA or AAA. Most have more than one farm club at the A level.

A good farm system produces quality players for the parent club and provides marketable players to offer in trades. A quality farm system is probably more important to clubs who have a difficult time competing in the free agent market.

Major-League Draft

This is the draft of minor-league players that's held at Baseball's Winter Meeting the first week in December. In this draft, major-league clubs can choose any unprotected player from another club's 40-man major-league roster, provided the player has three years of professional experience. The selection is similar to the amateur draft, in inverse order of the combined standings for both major leagues.

The drafting price is $25,000, but the club taking the player must keep him on its 25-man active roster the next season or offer to return him to his old club for $12,500.

No-Trade Clause

If this clause is written into a player's contract, the player may veto trades. Some players opt for a "limited no-trade clause," however, giving them the right to specify the clubs to which they would agree to be traded.

Option Year

This is the year a player's contract expires. During the option year, most players attempt to negotiate new contracts with their current clubs. If that fails, the option is played out and they file for free agency.

Optioned

A big-league club has a 40-man roster, but can keep only 25 on the active roster from the beginning of the season until Sept. 1. The other 15 players are *optioned* to the minor-league clubs and can be recalled after Sept. 1 without it counting as an additional option.

Outright Assignment

Instead of optioning a player to the minor leagues, a big-league club may choose to "outright" the player's contract to a farm club. In effect, the player is removed from the 40-man roster and must clear waivers before he can return to the club that previously held his contract.

Outright Release

This is what happens to a player who is fired by the club holding his contract. A player given the "pink slip" is free to negotiate a contract with any club willing to give him an opportunity.

Player Representative

A player representative represents his club as a member of the Player's Association governing body. This player, along with an alternate, is selected by his teammates.

Recall

When a player who had been optioned to the minor leagues is brought back to a major-league team, he is recalled.

Restrictive Rule

A player traded from one major-league club to another in the middle of a long-term contract can demand a trade at the end of the first year with his new club. For example, a player working on a five-year contract can invoke the restrictive rule if he is traded after the second year of that contract.

Scout

Each major-league club employs several individuals who **scout** for potential big-league ballplayers. Each scout is assigned a specific territory. He travels in his assigned area looking for available amateur talent.

A scout will watch a particular player on several occasions to evaluate his ability under game conditions. After a certain amount of observation, he will pass along his judgment of the player's ability to the club's director of scouting, who will evaluate the scout's report and make recommendations to the club's general manager. This information is then used to select players at the amateur draft.

Six-Year Rule

This is the minor-league version of the free agency system. A player who has been in the same club's farm system for six consecutive years, either at the major- or minor-league level, and not protected on the 40-man big-league roster, can declare himself a free agent. He is then in position to sign with any club that might desire his services.

Super Scout

He is the scout whose primary duty is to follow the other major-league clubs. He'll watch a particular player in order to recommend a potential trade to the general manager. He is also called on to analyze and evaluate strengths and weaknesses of future opponents. The information is used by the manager and coaches in establishing a strategy to use against the team.

Ten-and-Five Rule

A player who has spent 10 years in the major leagues, at least five with his present club, can veto any trade. Also, if he granted an unconditional release by the club holding his contract, he can reject a waiver claim from any other club. He then becomes a free agent and can sign with any club.

9
Umpires
and Rules

In how many sports can a manager or coach charge onto the playing area to protest a call without incurring a penalty? One of baseball's unique features is the nose-to-nose confrontation between a manager and umpire. Arguing with an umpire is a tradition in baseball.

There may be no tougher job in sports than being a baseball umpire. Every decision is in full view of countless critics, and his decision must be instantaneous. There is no replay for him to check. Once decided, it's history, and it's unpopular, he's going to hear about it — from the field as well as the stands.

In baseball, the manager may be allowed to run onto the field to protest or argue, but, in the end, it makes no difference — the umpire is always right, and no good umpire is going to change his call! Once a judgment is made, it stands.

Maybe because he knows every decision could draw the wrath of someone, the umpire tries to be as inconspicuous as possible on the field of play. Teddy Roosevelt probably didn't have umpires in mind when he said, "Walk quietly and carry a big stick," — but it fits!

This all leads to the reason the umpires are there in the first place: to enforce the rules of baseball. Obviously, a lot of judgment goes in to enforcing these rules, and given the number of decisions they make over the course of a game, umpires do a yeoman job.

What do you know about the rules of baseball? In this chapter you can test your understanding of the rules in the common, as well as the uncommon, situations. It will be a test for even the most astute baseball fan. And it will be great trivia material, regardless of how well-versed you are. We'll look at the rules right after a few questions and answers about umpires.

HOW ARE UMPIRES RECRUITED FOR THE MAJOR LEAGUES?

Just as the players do, umpires work their way up through the minor leagues. Most get their first job in the minor leagues after graduating from one of the many umpiring schools conducted by past and present big-league umpires. In the minors, umpires are scouted by major-league officials who look for such things as knowledge of rules, technique, mobility, consistency, judgment, and control of managers and players — even self-control.

Once an umpire reaches the majors, consistency is his ticket to staying there. Nowhere is consistency more important than in calling balls and strikes. As former umpiring great Bill Klem once said, "It's not only important that an umpire calls them like he sees them — he must call them correctly, too."

WHAT IS AN UMPIRE'S TOUGHEST CALL?

According to a survey of big-league umpires several year ago, calling balls and strikes presents them with their toughest calls. This is understandable when we realize the home plate umpire may have to make 200 ball-strike calls in a single game.

Of those calls, the most difficult may be the half-swing. On this play the umpire must decide if the batter had "an intent to swing," which results in a called strike; or if the batter's intent was not to swing, which results in a ball call. If the umpire rules the pitch a ball, the defensive team may request that the home plate umpire ask for help from either the first base or third base umpires. This is called an appeal play.

Once the home plate umpire receives a directive for an appeal from the defensive team, he will ask for help on the call from the third base umpire for a left-handed hitter or the first base umpire for a right-handed hitter. The reason it is handled this way is because the umpire opposite the side of the plate the batter swings has a better view of the batter's actions.

As soon as the appeal is made, the base umpire requested to make a decision will rule on the play. His decision is final. The base umpire's signal that the pitch is a ball is both arms spread parallel to the ground with palms facing down. One arm raised above his head with a closed fist signifies a strike.

It's important to note that a manager or coach cannot come out of the dugout to argue a ball or strike call. If he does, he is automatically ejected from the game.

Positioning is the key for the umpire to make the right call.

WHAT IS A "PHANTOM" DOUBLE PLAY?

One of the most difficult calls an umpire must make every day involves two separate, yet related calls. The first is the play where either the shortstop or second baseman "cheats" on what is called the "phantom" double play. The second is the call of runner interference for sliding out of the baseline at second base in an attempt to break up a double play.

A phantom double play happens when the infielder, attempting to pivot at second base and make a relay to first, throws the ball before touching the base or steps off the base before catching the ball to hasten his throw to first. The infielder "cheats" on this play to avoid the runner coming from first who wants to break up the double play. The runner is going to do everything he can to slide hard enough to try to knock the infielder out of the play, or at least knock him off balance on his throw to first.

In his desire to take the infielder out of the play, the runner may slide aggressively out of the baseline. In this case, the base runner aims for the infielder rather than the base in an attempt to break up the double play. If, in the umpire's judgment, the sliding runner is flagrantly out of the baseline, runner interference is called and both the runner going to second and batter-runner going to first are out.

It's not surprising that infielders try to avoid approaching runners by relaying the ball to first without actually touching the bag. Or they may tag the base a split-second before the throw arrives. In either situation, the pivot man is forced to fudge a little in order to stay out of the way of the incoming runner.

Did the shortstop touch the bag?

CAN ONE UMPIRE CHANGE ANOTHER UMPIRE'S DECISION?

Only if it involves an interpretation of the rules. If it's a judgment call, the only way a decision can be changed is if the umpire making the call requests assistance from another umpire who may have been in a better position to see the play.

WHY DOES THE UMPIRE TURN HIS BACK TO THE INFIELD WHEN CLEANING THE PLATE?

Tradition has it that this practice began as a courtesy to fans sitting behind home plate. With his back side facing the bleachers in center field, the home plate umpire was not as offensive to the fans sitting out there as he was to those sitting right behind home plate.

I remember once, while on the pitching mound, seeing the home plate umpire's pants rip while dusting off the plate. What a ribbing he would have taken if facing the other way, right?

WHY DO MANAGERS OR REPRESENTATIVES FOR EACH TEAM MEET WITH THE UMPIRES AT HOME PLATE BEFORE EACH GAME?

The teams exchange batting orders and submit two copies of their lineup cards to the home plate umpire at this meeting. The umpire checks the batting orders on the cards for accuracy and technical errors — for instance, a player being included twice or an inaccurate number of player listed in the starting lineup. Once the umpire accepts the cards, he keeps one copy from each club and gives each club representative a copy of the other club's lineup card. At this point, no changes can be made in the batting order except by substitution.

Prior to the first game of a series, the home manager will review the ground rules pertinent to the home park during this meeting. All ballparks are not built exactly alike, making it necessary to establish ground rules for certain situations that affect play. These rules are communicated by the home club's manager or representative to both the umpire crew and visiting club's representative.

An example of an unusual ground rule can be found in San Diego's Jack Murphy Stadium. If a fair ball rolls under the bullpen bench it's in play and the runner may advance as many bases as possible.

WHAT IS THE PURPOSE OF THE INFIELD FLY RULE?

An infield fly is a pop-up in fair territory which can be caught by an infielder when at least first and second base are occupied, and there are less than two outs. When it's apparent to the umpire that an infielder will make a play on the ball, he immediately shouts, "Infield fly," or "Infield fly, if fair," if the pop-up is near the foul line. The batter is automatically out at this point. The runners may advance at their own risk if the ball is misplayed and drops safely to the ground in fair territory.

The infield fly rule prevents an infielder from intentionally dropping a pop-up with two or more runners on base for the purpose of getting a double play. Since the runners have to remain near the bag on a fly ball, turning a double play off a pop-up would be a rather easy task.

THERE HAS BEEN A LOT OF TALK ABOUT THE BASEBALL BEING "LIVELIER." IS THIS POSSIBILE? WHAT RULES GOVERN BALL PRODUCTION?

Tests results show the only real change in official baseballs over the past 40 years is the cover. In my playing days it was made of horsehide, but cowhide became the official cover in 1975.

Production of a ball begins with a rubber-coated cork center, followed by three layers of wool yarn tightly wound by machine. The final touch is a personal one. Eighty-eight inches of waxed thread rolled to a consistent surface are used to make 108 red stitches on each ball. The stitches are sewn by hand and flattened by a rolling machine to provide consistency in height. Each ball must weigh between 5 and $5^{1}/_{4}$ ounces and measure between 9 and $9^{1}/_{4}$ inches in diameter.

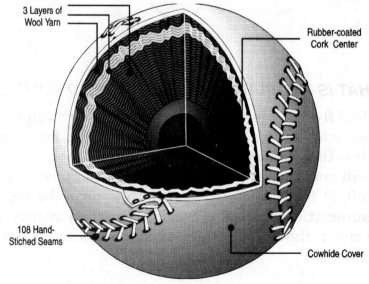

3 Layers of Wool Yarn

Rubber-coated Cork Center

108 Hand-Stiched Seams

Cowhide Cover

A random sampling of balls in each shipment from the factory is tested for "statistical accuracy." In these tests, balls are shot from a cannon at a wall of white ash, the same wood from which bats are made. The striking and rebounding velocity of each ball is measured. Results are recapped in a ratio called the Coefficient of Restitution (COR). This ratio must be in a specific range to meet major-league standards.

Either major league reserves the right to call for an independent test of balls at any time. This is a constraint to any attempts to create a livelier or "juiced" ball.

WHAT IS THE RULING WHEN THE DESIGNATED HITTER IS INSERTED IN A DEFENSIVE POSITION?

The designated hitter bats for the starting pitcher and all subsequent pitchers in a game. When the designated hitter replaces a fielder in the lineup during the game, he continues to bat in the same spot in the batting order. The pitcher in the game at that point must hit in place of the player the designated hitter replaced.

WHAT CONSTITUTES RUNNER INTERFERENCE?

There are four situations where runner interference can be called by the umpire:

1) When a runner collides with a fielder making an effort to field a batted ball, except when the runner is legally on base when the interference occurs.

2) A runner throws his hands up and intentionally changes the course of a thrown ball.

3) A runner intentionally interferes with a batted ball for the purpose of preventing a possible double play.

4) A runner, in an attempt to break up a double play, slides wide of the bag intentionally trying to take the pivot man out of the play.

Number 4 occurs most often during a game. On this, or any other interference call with less than two outs, both the runner and batter are called out.

WHAT CONSTITUTES A BALK?

It is a balk when the pitcher:

- Fails to come to a complete stop in the set position (with runners on the bases).
- While on the pitching rubber, fakes throwing to first base.
- While on the pitching rubber, throws or fakes a throw to an unoccupied base except for the purpose of making a play.
- While on the pitching rubber, fails to step toward the base to which he is throwing.
- While on the pitching rubber, makes any pitching motion without making a pitch.
- Makes an illegal pitch.
- Unnecessarily delays the game.
- When in the set position, makes any movement of the body except the head.
- When in the set position, steps off the pitching rubber without separating the ball from his glove.
- Pitches when he's not facing the batter.
- When in the set position, takes one hand off the ball without throwing.
- Drops the ball while on the pitching rubber.
- Pitches when the catcher is not in the catcher's box.
- Stands on or aside the rubber without the ball.

WHAT DO YOU KNOW ABOUT THE RULES OF BASEBALL?

Now it is your turn to be the umpire. What is your call on these 12 rules situations?

1) With a runner on second base, the pitcher takes his stretch and glances back at the runner. As the pitcher turns back toward home plate to start his delivery, the batter has reached over to pick up some dirt. In his confusion, the pitcher stops his delivery and fails to make the pitch. Is it a balk?

2) The bases are loaded in the bottom of the ninth inning in a 6-6 game. The batter is walked, forcing in a potentially winning run from third base. The batter trots down and touches first base as the runner from third crosses home plate. But in the excitement, the runner on first base fails to touch second base, rushing instead to congratulate his teammates. The defensive team tosses the ball to the shortstop who steps on second base. Is the runner who fails to touch second the third out or does the winning run score?

3) With two outs and a runner on first base, the batter hits a scorcher up the middle, striking the leg of the umpire who is on the infield grass. The ball deflects to the shortstop who steps on second base for a force out. Is the runner out or is the ball dead with the runner at first advanced to second and the batter awarded first base?

4) The batter hits a dribbler down the first base line in fair territory. As the batter breaks for first, the catcher is right behind him in hot pursuit of the ball. Just as the batter reaches the position of the ball it crosses over into foul territory. Wanting to ensure that the ball remains in foul territory, the batter-runner kicks the ball toward the dugout. Is the batter-runner out for interfering with a foul ball?

5) There is a runner at third base and one out. The game is tied 2-2 in the seventh inning. The No. 8 hitter is at bat. Sensing a squeeze play, the pitcher, after coming to his set position, quickly steps back off the pitching rubber as the runner on third prematurely breaks for home plate. The pitcher fires the ball toward the plate, where the batter lays down a perfect squeeze bunt. Is it a legally bunted ball?

6) A left-handed pitcher with a good screwball is on the mound. A switch-hitter, batting right-handed, swings and misses the first pitch. Deciding that he may have more success against the screwball from the left side of the plate, he immediately switches over. Can he switch sides during the same time at bat?

7) With a runner on first base, the pitcher takes his stretch and delivers the ball to home plate without coming to a set position. By the time the third base umpire raises his arms and yells out "Balk!" the ball is in flight toward home plate. Unaware of the balk call, the batter swings and lines a single to left field. Is the ball dead when the umpire rules a balk? Or is the batter credited with a base hit, allowing him to remain at first with the runner advancing as many bases as possible?

8) With runners on first and second and one out, the batter lifts a high pop-up halfway to first base near the foul line. The umpire yells, "Infield fly, if fair!" The first baseman charges in and appears to be in a position to catch the ball. However, he overruns the ball and it lands behind him, hits the edge of the grass and trickles into foul territory. Is the infield fly rule still in effect?

9) Runners are on first and second with no one out. The batter lifts a high pop fly into short right field. As the second baseman camps under the ball waiting for its descent, the umpire rules an infield fly automatically retiring the batter. At the last moment the second baseman loses the ball in the sun, and it falls safely to the ground. The runner on second base, standing about 10 feet off the base, immediately breaks for third base. The second baseman retrieves the ball and throws it across the diamond to the third baseman, who stretches out to receive the throw just ahead of the sliding runner. Did the runner need to tag up before advancing? Is it a tag play or force out?

10) With two outs a pinch hitter swings and misses a low curve ball for the third strike. The catcher, thinking he had caught the ball before it touched the ground for the third out, rolls the ball out toward the pitching mound and retreats toward his dugout. As the pinch hitter heads back toward his dugout, his teammates notice that the umpire has not called him out, and frantically urge him to run to first base. Stopping just short of the dugout, he turns and races toward first, reaching the base safely. Is he out for running out of the baseline? Or is he safe?

11) The batter lifts a high pop-up along the third base line. The third baseman misjudges the ball and it lands behind him in foul territory, about halfway between third and home. The ball then bounces into fair territory where it comes to rest. Is the call "fair" or "foul?"

12) There is a runner on first base and two strikes on the batter. As the pitcher delivers the ball, the runner breaks for second base on a hit-and-run play. The hitter, in an attempt to protect the runner, swings at a fast ball and misses, but the ball hits him. Is the batter entitled to take his base or is he out? If he is out, what happens to the runner?

ANSWERS

1) Maybe yes. Maybe no. The call depends on the umpire's judgment, or more precisely, his ability to read minds. If the act by the batter is judged unintentional, a balk is called on the pitcher. If in the opinion of the umpire it was an intentional act, the batter is subject to ejection from the game.

2) The run scores. The Rule Book states, "The umpire shall not declare the game ended until the runner forced to advance from third has touched home plate and the batter-runner has touched first base." No mention is made of the other two runners.

3) No one is out. The ball becomes dead when it touches an umpire in fair territory and before it passes either first or third base. The runners advance one base, and the batter goes to first base.

4) The batter is out. According to the Rule Book, "A batter is out after hitting or bunting a foul ball if he intentionally deflects the course of the ball in any manner while running to first."

5) No. Once the pitcher steps off the pitching rubber, he becomes an infielder and his throw to the plate is not a legal pitch. The runner is out and the batter continues to hit.

6) He can as long as he steps from one batter's box to another before the pitcher is ready to pitch.

7) When a balk is called, the play is not necessarily over. Play continues without the balk being recognized if the batter reaches base in any manner. But if he should be put out or fail to hit the ball in fair territory, the pitch is disallowed and the runner awarded second base.

8) No. It's foul. Remember the umpire's call, "Infield fly, if fair."

9) The runner is not required to tag up. Since the batter is already out, it's a tag play instead of a force out. The runner is safe.

10) If first base is unoccupied with less than two outs or occupied with two outs, a batter who misses a third strike and the umpire does not signal that the ball has been legally caught by the catcher, may attempt to reach first base from any point prior to reaching the dugout. He is safe unless tagged or thrown out by the catcher.

11) It's a fair ball.

12) The batter is out, the ball is dead and the runner returns to first base.

WHAT OTHER RULINGS MIGHT INTEREST A MORE ASTUTE FAN?

- The pine tar placed on the bat handle to improve the grip cannot extend more than 18 inches from the knob end of the bat. The George Brett incident a few seasons back brought this rule to the forefront.

- The pitcher's glove must be one color, but not be white or gray because these colors are similar to the ball's color.

- A pitcher is allotted eight warm-up pitches on the mound before each inning or after coming in as a reliever, with one exception — when a pitcher is called into the game to replace an injured pitcher the reliever is allowed as much warm-up time as needed.

- If a pitcher goes to his mouth with his throwing hand while on the mound, the umpire will immediately call a ball on the batter.

- If a batter swings and misses or takes a third strike and it eludes the catcher, the batter may not attempt to reach first base if that base is occupied with fewer than two outs. If the base is unoccupied or there are two outs, the batter is safe if he reaches first before the catcher can retrieve the ball and make a play.

- A manager is prohibited from arguing a ball or strike call. If he leaves the dugout to argue a call, he receives a warning to return to the dugout. An unheeded warning will result in his ejection from the game.

10
Averages,
Records and
Awards

Baseball is a game of numbers and records. What happens on the field is statistically recorded for each player. In fact, no other sport keeps such a large array of statistics.

Perhaps the reason baseball keeps such a detailed account of what happens on the field is the focus on the individual player. A player's every action is out in the open for all to see. What happened, happened.

Small wonder that fans single out statistics for special attention. The amount of memorabilia collected by baseball buffs is symbolic of this obsession with averages, percentages and records.

With baseball's strong emphasis on numbers, it's only natural that there are many individual awards. Players with the best statistics during the season — and their careers — are in line to be recognized for their efforts.

But how are these averages and percentages? Which ones determine a player's true effectiveness for his club? How are individual awards determined? This chapter centers on what goes into the numbers and what the numbers mean to the player, his teammates and the fans.

HOW ARE AVERAGES AND PERCENTAGES THAT DETERMINE A HITTER'S PERFORMANCE LEVEL FIGURED?

Batting Average

A player's batting average is determined by dividing the number of official appearances at bat into the number of hits. Example: A player with 180 hits in 600 plate appearances has a batting average of .300 by dividing the number of official plate appearances (600) into the number of hits (180).

A batter is credited with an official at bat when he hits a ball that results in a hit, force play, fielder's choice or error, or if he strikes out, grounds out or flys out. When a player walks, reaches base on catcher's interference, is hit by a pitch, or credited with a sacrafice, he is not charged with an official at bat.

To win a batting championship, a hitter must average 3.1 plate appearances each game on the schedule. At the major-league level, a player must have 502 plate appearances (3.1 times 162 games).

Runs Batted In (RBIs)

RBIs indicate a player's ability to score teammates. When a run scores as a direct result of the batter's hit, ground ball, sacrifice fly, walk or being hit by a pitch, the batter is credited with an RBI. The batter does not get credit for an RBI if a run scores while he grounds into a double play. He also may not get credit for an RBI if there is an error on the play. If the official scorer judges the run would have scored regardless of the error, the batter is awarded an RBI.

Slugging Percentage

Slugging percentage is figured by adding the number of bases a batter reaches on hits — a single counts one, double two, triple three, home run four. This number is divided by the number of official times at bat. Example: a player who has 600 official times at bat and is credited with 360 total bases has a slugging percentage of .600 (360 divided by 600).

This statistic demonstrates a hitter's ability to generate extra-base hits. To qualify for the slugging percentage title, a player must have 3.1 official plate appearances for each game, the same as for the batting title.

On Base Percentage

This average points out offensive contributions of singles-type hitters who do what is necessary to get on base. The on base percentage is figured by finding the number of times a batter reaches base hits, walks, errors, being hit by a pitch or catcher's interference. This number is divided by the number of plate appearances. Example: A player who reaches base 250 times in 600 at bats has an on base percentage of .400 (250 divided by 600).

Batting Average with Runners in Scoring Position

You won't find this unofficial statistic in the record books. Nevertheless, it has gained a great deal of respect in recent years because it's useful in identifying the hitters on a team who are good in clutch situations. How did the hitter fare with a runner or runners on second or third, or second and third, or, to ask it another way, did he hit well with runners in scoring position? Another version is to determine a hitter's batting average with two outs and runners in scoring position. This is the epitome of clutch hitting.

HOW ARE PITCHERS' AND FIELDERS' AVERAGES DETERMINED?

Earned Run Average (ERA)

An earned run is a one that scores as a result of a base hit, base on balls or wild pitch. If an error or passed ball by the catcher contributes to a run or prolongs an inning, the run and subsequent runs are unearned and not charged to the pitcher. A pitcher's ERA is found by multiplying the number of earned runs he has allowed by nine (number of innings in a game). This is divided by the total number of innings pitched. Example: a pitcher has allowed 80 earned runs in 200 innings. The formula is 80 times 9 equals 720 divided by 200 (innings pitched). The answer is an ERA of 3.60. In other words, the pitcher has allowed an average of 3.6 runs for every nine innings pitched.

To qualify for the ERA title, a pitcher must pitch at least as many innings as the number of games scheduled that season. For a big-league pitcher that number is 162.

Saves

This demonstrates a relief pitcher's effectiveness. A save is awarded when he enters the game and finds the potential tying or winning run on base or at the plate, or he pitches at least three or more effective innings and holds a lead. The relief pitcher must complete the game to earn a save.

Fielding Average

A player's fielding average is computed by adding the number of putouts, assists and errors recorded by the player while in the field. Divide the sum of putouts and assists by the former number. Example: A player has 200 putouts, 100 assists and 10 errors, which add up to 310. The total number of putouts and assists is 300. Three hundred divided by 310 results in a fielding average of .970.

The individual fielding champion at each position is the player with the highest fielding average who appears in at least two-thirds of the scheduled games at that position except catcher. A catcher must appear behind the plate in at least half of the scheduled games to qualify. At the major-league level, an infielder or outfielder must participate in 108 games at his position. A catcher must appear in 81.

HOW ARE VARIOUS INDIVIDUAL AWARDS DETERMINED?

Hall of Fame

This is the epitome of recognition for a player. Voting for the Baseball Hall of Fame is done by members of the Baseball Writers Association of America (BBWAA). To be included on the ballot, a player must have played in the major leagues 10 years and been out of baseball as an active player at least five years.

To be elected, a player must receive votes on at least 75 percent of the returned ballots by BBWAA members. Once a player appears on the ballot, he remains on it every year for 15 years. His name will be removed if he is elected or receives votes on less than five percent of the ballots returned.

Most Valuable Player (MVP)

This is the top individual award for performance in a single season. Two BBWAA members from each major-league city vote for the MVP. Each writer ranks the 10 top players in his respective league, with the top player on his list receiving 10 points. The second player on the list receives nine points, the third eight, and so on. The player with the highest point total is the MVP. An MVP is selected in both the National and American Leagues.

In making their determination, BBWAA participating members review offensive and defensive statistics of the top players in their respective leagues. The lack of defensive statistics is the primary reason a designated hitter has failed to win the MVP.

Cy Young Award

This annual award goes to the best pitcher in the American and National Leagues as selected by the BBWAA. Voting is similar to the method used for the MVP.

In selecting the season's best pitchers, the writers look for such things as won-loss percentage, ERA, strikeout-to-walk ratio, hits allowed per nine innings, innings pitched (by a starting pitcher), saves (relief pitcher) and if he pitched for a divisional or pennant winner.

Rookie of the Year

This award, voted on by BBWAA members, goes to the best first-year performers in each major league. To qualify, a player must not have made more than 130 trips to home plate, pitched more than 50 innings or spent more than 45 days on a major-league roster during the 25-player limit from the beginning of the season to August 31.

Gold Glove Award

This is the all-star fielding team. In each league, managers and coaches select the player from each defensive position they consider the supreme performers. Managers and coaches may not vote for players on their own club.

The award is based on overall fielding excellence, including fielding percentage, assists, putouts and a penchant for making big plays.

HOW IS THE NUMBER OF GAMES
A TEAM IS OUT OF FIRST PLACE DETERMINED?

Each win and each loss count as one-half game. If a club is seven games out of first place, it must not only win seven in a row, the first-place team must lose seven straight before the teams will be tied. If the first-place club loses four of seven, the second-place team is still three games behind.

When first- and second-place clubs play each other, each game is worth a two-game swing. For example, if the second-place club is three games back in the standings and beats the first-place club, it is then two games out of first place. But if the second-place club loses, it falls four games behind, a two-game swing in the standings.

AS THE PENNANT RACE HEATS UP, A TEAM'S "MAGIC NUMBER"
IS OFTEN GIVEN. WHAT DOES IT MEAN?

The "magic number" is the combination of wins needed by the first-place club and losses by its closest opponent for the leading team to win the pennant.

The magic number is determined by taking the number of games the first-place team has left to play, adding one to that figure, then subtracting the number of games the club is ahead of the nearest opponent in the loss column of the league standings. For example: Club A has nine games left on its schedule and leads Club B by three games in the loss column. Nine (games left) plus one is 10; subtract three (games back) for a magic number of seven. In numerical form it looks like this:

$$9 + 1 = 10 - 3 = 7$$

Late in the season as the pennant comes to a climax, games in the loss column take on more importance. The reason is Club B could be three games behind in the standings but only one behind in the loss column. This would mean that the Club A has five more wins while playing four more games than Club B. The numbers would look like this:

	W	**L**
Club A	88	73
Club B	83	74

Since Club B has played four less games, it still has a chance to win those games, giving it an opportunity to make up some deficit with Club A. Because of this, the loss column tells the bigger story down the stretch. Once a game is in the loss column, there is no way to make it up.

WHAT STATISTIC SAYS THE MOST
ABOUT A HITTER'S EFFECTIVENESS?

A hitter's batting averages, on-base percentages, slugging percentages and RBIs are all important statistics. But none of them alone tells the story. What does a batting average tell us? Does it tell us when the hits were made? How effective were the hits? Did they help start some offensive rallies? Did they advance a large percentage of runners along on the base paths? Did they drive home a few important or winning runs?

How and when did the batter get on base? Does he have a history of getting on base when the game is on the line? Or does he seem to be more effective in those at bats when the pressure is not on because his club is way ahead or way behind in the score?

For the batter with the big slugging percentage, did a significant portion of that heavy slugging come in important situations? In other words, can he deliver the big double, triple or home run when the chips are down? As for RBIs, when did they come? Did the batter drive in eight runs in two games and then draw a blank for six games? Or did he drive in eight runs in seven of those eight games? The real question is: how consistent was he with runners in scoring position in clutch situations?

When the hits come is more meaningful and more indicative of a batter's worth to his ballclub. Another way to put it: is the player a tough out when it counts?

WHAT ARE THE DUTIES OF THE OFFICIAL SCORER?

Baseball is the only game which requires an individual — the official scorer — to determine the scoring on a particular play. For example, on a hard-hit ball that skips off the third baseman's glove to score a run, the official scorer will rule whether it is a hit or error. This ruling will in turn determine if the run is earned or unearned.

The official scorer at each major-league stadium is appointed to that position by the league president. Normally, the official scorer is either an active or retired sportswriter and a member of the Baseball Writers of America Association (BBWAA).

As the game progresses, the official scorer will keep a detailed record of the action on the field in the official scorebook. The box score, the published summary of the game, comes from this information.

WHAT IS THE TRIPLE CROWN?

A player who leads his league in batting average, home runs and RBIs during the same season wins the Triple Crown. Winning the Triple Crown requires power and the ability to hit for average — rare attributes in today's players. The last player to win the Triple Crown was Carl Yastrzemski of the Boston Red Sox in 1967.

WHAT DOES IT MEAN TO "HIT FOR THE CYCLE?"

A batter who hits a single, double, triple and home run in the same game has hit for the cycle. At the big-league level, this is rare. The most it has been accomplished in one season is three times. Several players have accomplished this.

It's worth mentioning that the toughest hit in completing the cycle is the triple. What makes it more difficult than the others is that it requires both speed and power — a rare combination.

11
Extra
Innings

Baseball. The National Pastime. Apple pie. Mom. Hot dogs.

Nothing better defines the American way than big-league baseball, this kids' game played by men. As we head toward the end of the game, I will cover two general questions that are indicative of baseball's role in our culture. These questions didn't seem to fit anywhere else in the scheme of things, but I wanted to get them in the game.

The questions:

- "What is it about this grand old game of baseball that has made it a part of the fabric of our existence?"
- "What role has baseball played in the development of our language?"

I'll close with that great American classic made famous by the comedy team of Bud Abbott and Lou Costello, *Who's on First?* With this final pitch, let me tell you that I have enjoyed spending this time with you. It was fun for me, and I hope it was fun for you.

WHAT IS IT ABOUT THIS GRAND OLD GAME OF BASEBALL THAT HAS MADE IT A PART OF THE FABRIC OF OUR EXISTENCE?

I doubt that you have stopped anyone at work lately and told him that baseball's very essence combines three deep-seated human instincts — to run, to throw and to strike. Through untold periods of time, survival of the human race depended on the ability to run the fastest, throw the straightest and strike the hardest.

Even though these instincts are no longer conditions of survival, they still are part of our nature. After ages of mental evolution, we still have an appetite for these forms of behavior in spectator form.

Consider these game situations: your favorite club has the potential winning run on third base. When the batter steps into the box, who is there with him? When the bases are loaded, who hurls a high, hard fastball to a dangerous hitter just as surely as the pitcher does? When a slow-footed runner rounds third base and heads for home plate with a crucial run, who is stride-by-stride with the runner, hustling to beat the throw from center field? Part of being a real fan is feeling you have contributed your own energies to your team's cause.

Baseball Is a Constant

One of the more positive things baseball has offered through the years is consistency in the midst of a world of change. Someone once remarked, "Some things are forever changing, yet they always seem to remain the same." Baseball is that way. It has changed, but for the most part the changes have been gradual, if not reluctant, in coming.

Probably the biggest changes, as we saw in an earlier chapter, are those that have taken place off the field. As noted in Chapter 8, baseball is now a big business. Salaries have soared, management and the players union seem to be forever at odds and a strike always appears to be just around the corner. But that's another story.

On the field, baseball has not been changed by a lot of rules. We know the game we see season after season will be familiar. Perhaps the words of noted sportswriter Furman Bisher best sum up the feeling a lot of us have about baseball's consistency: "It (baseball) has guarded fervently its heritage. Its standards have been preserved. Baseball hasn't fallen in with the rest of society and compromised tradition, and thrown principle to the wind."

Pace Appeal

Another attraction of baseball that captures hearts and minds is the pace of the game. There was a time, not many years ago, when baseball was the facsimile of life itself. Most Americans lived on farms or in small towns, where the pace of life was slow and thorough, if not leisurely. Times are different now. We live and work in a complex, hurry-up world. The pace has quickened, the pressure intensified.

Baseball's appeal continues to be its representation of a slower pace of life, a return to a time when things were not moving so rapidly. The one great elemental fact about baseball is that there is a lot of inaction. For many of us, that still counts for something. The ballpark offers a place to get away from the high-pressure grind of daily living. Somehow it makes the task of "survival" in the real world a little easier.

Unpredictable

The unexpected is another prime facet of baseball's absorbing interest. When we buy a ticket, we don't know what kind of game we'll see. On any given night, there can be a wide spectrum of emotions — from a tight game where beads of sweat break across our brows to a game where our favorites need a half-dozen runs in the ninth to win.

Experiencing emotional reactions is part of being a baseball fan. Our emotions range from applause and cheers, to boos and jeers. In other words, if the job is being done, we cheer. If it isn't, most of us voice our displeasure by booing.

Baseball is many things to a real fan, but it's never dull.

Always There

Baseball is always there. It goes beyond the calendar. It's not only on view from Opening Day to the World Series, but it rests comfortably on our tongues through the winter, keeping our interest alive.

In what some of us old-timers call the "Hot Stove League," we share with other baseball enthusiasts the "what-ifs" and "buts" of the past season. We also ponder the "maybes" and "possibilities" of the coming season. Add a trade or two and the suspense of free agency, and there is enough fuel to keep the fire burning right up to the first crack of the bat in the spring.

Then comes spring training. We get wrapped up in news of our favorite club as it prepares for the coming season. "This is the year!" "We can win it!" "We are much improved!" It makes little difference that we pull for a club that is rarely a winner — that our favorite club has been "a going-nowhere" club for years — this is a new season with new hopes and expectations. We eagerly await the umpire's cry of "Play ball!"

Then when the season begins, we are right back in there cheering and booing, sweating and straining, rooting and pulling for our favorite clubs. And the cycle continues — season after season.

WHAT BASEBALL TERMS HAVE BECOME PART OF OUR EVERYDAY LANGUAGE?

We only have to look at our language to appreciate how much baseball has woven itself into the fabric of our culture. In everyday conversations we use a great number of phrases and words derived from baseball terminology. Many of these are so firmly entrenched that they are acceptable in the most conservative speaking situations.

Most of us understand and use terms like:

- Someone else has the lead, but you are in there to **BACK UP HIS PLAY.**
- To do something in a special way is to be **BIG LEAGUE.**
- A deed that is crude or cheap stamps someone as **BUSH (LEAGUE).**
- A surprising development often finds you **CAUGHT OFF BASE.**
- To cover all the possibilities is to **COVER ALL THE BASES.**
- To be alert is to have your **EYE ON THE BALL.**
- An obnoxious, loud person is a **FOUL BALL.**
- To understand a situation is to **GET THE PITCH.**
- To fail from the start means you don't **GET TO FIRST BASE.**
- When you fail to get discouraged, it's because you know you will **GET YOUR TURN AT BAT.**
- To stand up for someone is to **GO TO BAT** for him.
- To do something solely for attention is to make a **GRAND-STAND PLAY.**
- When responsibility lies in your hands, you **HAVE THE BALL.**
- Something that stands out to you is a **HIT.**
- When you have done your best, you are probably **HOME SAFE.**

- When you are doing your duty, you are *IN THERE PITCHING.*
- To lose out is to be *KNOCKED OUT OF THE BOX.*
- When you have something to sell, you *MAKE YOUR PITCH.*
- To be unprepared often results in your being *OUT IN LEFT FIELD.*
- To take on a task for which you have little knowledge may leave you *OUT OF YOUR LEAGUE.*
- To come to someone's aid in an emergency is to *PINCH HIT* for him.
- To postpone an invitation to a later date is to ask for a *RAINCHECK.*
- A big mistake is a *REAL BLOOPER.*
- An accurate and true statement is *RIGHT DOWN THE MIDDLE.*
- To pick something up quickly is to get it *RIGHT OFF THE BAT.*
- If you have unusual ideas and beliefs you may be referred to as a *SCREWBALL.*
- To come up empty-handed is to be *SHUT OUT.*
- When you are caught in the middle, you may be the victim of a *SQUEEZE PLAY.*
- To get it together is to have *SOMETHING ON THE BALL.*
- To try something and fail is to *STRIKE OUT.*
- To be misled is to be *THROWN A CURVE.*
- When you are confronted with obstacles from the start, you have *TWO STRIKES AGAINST YOU.*
- Until you get going, you are just *WARMING UP.*
- To be indiscreet is to be *WAY OFF BASE.*
- When someone is ready to go along, he is *WILLING TO PLAY BALL.*

WHO'S ON FIRST?

Here is the famous Bud Abbott-Lou Costello routine:

Costello: Hey, Abbott, tell me the names of the players on our baseball team so I can say hello to them.

Abbott: Sure, WHO'S on first, WHAT'S on second, I-DON'T-KNOW's on third...

Costello: Now, wait. What's the name of the first baseman?

Abbott: No, WHAT'S the name of the second baseman.

Costello: I DON'T KNOW.

Abbott: He's the third baseman.

Costello: Let's start over.

Abbott: OK, WHO'S on first...

Costello: I'm asking you, what's the name of the first baseman?

Abbott: WHAT'S the name of the second baseman.

Costello: I DON'T KNOW.

Abbott: He's on third.

Costello: All I'm trying to find out is the name of the first baseman.

Abbott: I keep telling you, WHO'S on first.

Costello: I'm asking YOU what's the name of the first baseman.

Abbott: (Rapidly) WHAT'S the name of the second baseman.

Costello: (More rapidly) I DON'T KNOW.

Both: (Most rapidly) Third base!!

Costello: All right. OK. You won't tell what's the name of the first baseman.

Abbott: I've been telling you. WHAT'S the name of the second baseman.

Costello: I'm asking you, who's on second?

Abbott: WHO'S on first.

Costello: I don't know.

Abbott: He's on third.

Costello: Let's do it this way. You pay the players on this team?

Abbott: Absolutely.

Costello: All right. Now, when you give the first baseman his paycheck, who gets the money?

Abbott: Every penny of it.

Costello: WHO?

Abbott: Naturally.

Costello: Naturally?

Abbott: Of course.

Costello: All right. Then Naturally's on first...

Abbott: No. WHO'S on first.

Costello: I'm asking you! What's the name of the first baseman?

Abbott: And I'm telling you! WHAT'S the name of the second baseman.

Costello: You say, third base, I'll.... (Pause) Wait a minute. You got a pitcher on this team?

Abbott: Did you ever hear of a team without a pitcher?

Costello: All right. Tell me the pitcher's name.

Abbott: TOMORROW.

Costello: You want to tell me now?

Abbott: I said I'd tell you: TOMORROW.

Costello: What's wrong with today?

Abbott: NOTHING. He's a pretty good catcher.

Costello: Who's the catcher?

Abbott: No. WHO'S the first baseman.

Costello: All right, tell me: What's the first baseman's name?

Abbott: No, WHAT'S the second baseman's name.

Costello: I-don't-know?

Abbott: Look, it's very simple.

Costello: I know it's simple. You got a pitcher. TOMORROW. He throws the ball to TODAY. TODAY throws the ball to WHO, he throws the ball to WHAT, WHAT throws the ball to I-DON'T-KNOW, he's on third...and what's more, I-DON'T-GIVE-A-DARN!

Abbott: What's that?

Costello: I said, I-Don't-Give-A-Darn.

Abbott: Oh, he's our shortstop.

Glossary

AT BAT

Batting Gloves — Special gloves worn by the hitter to enhance the grip on the bat and reduce the sting of the ball when it's not hit on the fat part of the bat.

Deep in the Box — Refers to the hitter who stands away from the plate with his back foot on or near the back line of the batter's box. This allows him to see the ball longer and be more selective in the pitches he attempts to hit. The disadvantage of standing deep in the box is having to swing at a breaking pitch after it has made its break.

Doughnut — Weighted metal ring slipped onto the bat barrel by the on-deck hitter. The additional weight helps loosen his muscles and as he takes practice swings in the on-deck circle and makes the bat feel lighter when he is at the plate.

Opposite-Field Hitter — A batter who often hits the ball to the side of the field opposite his natural side — right field for a right-handed hitter or left field for a left-handed batter. This type of hitter waits longer for the ball, enabling him to be more selective in the pitches he attempts to hit. Opposite-field hitters seldom strike out, nor do they hit a lot of home runs.

Protecting the Plate — With two strikes on him, the good hitter gives in a bit and shortens his swing, trying to just meet the ball and put it in play. When a batter does this he is protecting the plate.

Protecting the Runner — On a steal attempt, the batter swings and purposely misses the pitch to try to distract the catcher and briefly delay his throw to the base. By protecting the runner in this manner, the batter gives the runner a better chance of stealing the base.

Pull Hitter —The batter who consistently hits the ball to his natural side of the field — a right-handed batter hits the ball to the left side of the field, the left-handed batter to the right. To pull the ball, the batter must have quick wrists and fast hip rotation. This enables him to hit the ball at the earliest possible moment and pull it.

Rolling — Descriptive of the method taught to hitters for getting out of the way of high inside pitches. Rolling is executed by a quick quarter turn of the upper body and head away from the pitch.

Sacrifice Bunt — On a sacrifice bunt, the batter gives himself up, or sacrifices himself, to move the runner or runners up a base. It's more difficult to execute on artificial surface than natural grass because the hardness of the artificial surface makes it tougher to deaden the ball if the bunted ball hits on the artificial surface first. To successfully execute the sacrifice bunt, the bunter will try to make sure the ball hits first in the small dirt portion in front of home plate.

Straightaway Hitter — This type of hitter uses the whole field by hitting the ball where it is pitched. By going with the pitch in this manner, the straightaway hitter is rarely fooled on the pitch, makes more consistent contact and doesn't strike out as often as the pull hitter. Most batters with high lifetime batting averages are straightaway hitters. A significant reason for this is their ability to hit to all fields making them tough to defend.

Up the Alley — Extra-base hit between either the right fielder and center fielder or the left fielder and center fielder. Also referred to as a "tweener."

BASERUNNING

Caught Leaning — In his haste to get a good jump toward the next base, a base runner may "lean" in that direction. This provides an advantage to the runner if the pitcher delivers the ball to the plate. It may prove to be a disadvantage if the pitcher attempts a pickoff because the runner is leaning away from the bag and may not be able to get back safely.

Double Steal — When two runners steal bases on the same play. It most often takes place with runners at first and third. In this situation, the runner on first attempts to steal second base with the intent of drawing a late throw from the catcher. The runner on third breaks for home and beats the return throw home as the catcher's throw goes through to second base. If both runners are safe, they have successfully executed a double steal.

Halfway — On a fly ball not deep enough for him to tag up and advance to the next base, the runner will move halfway to the next base and await the results of the play. He will only move far enough toward the next base to be able to safely return when the ball is caught.

One Base at a Time — When behind by several runs late in the game, a base runner does not want to be thrown out trying to take an extra base or being doubled up on a line drive hit to an infielder. What his club needs is base runners and runs. The best strategy calls for the runner to play it safe and move up one base at a time.

Pinch Runner — Replaces a runner on base. The man taken out can't return to the game, but the pinch runner may stay in the game.

Scoring Position — A runner on second or third base is in scoring position.

Tag Up — The third base coach's instruction to a runner on third base when a fly ball is hit by the batter with less than two outs. The runner can advance if he has one foot on the base when the ball is caught. Smart runners on first or second will tag up on long fly balls and be in position to advance. Tagging up at first base is a common practice on a fly ball with a runner on third and less than two outs. In this situation if the throw goes through to the plate, the runner on first most likely can move up to second.

Wide Turn at First — A wider than normal turn at first base after a batter hits a single. This puts him in position to continue to second if the outfielder misplays the ball.

Wrong Turn — A batter-runner can legally overrun first base. Contrary to popular belief, he can remain in fair territory after he has passed the bag. If he turns to his left or makes any kind of movement toward second base, he has made a wrong turn and can be put out if tagged by a fielder before returning to first base or reaching second base safely.

PITCHING

Backing Up — With runners on base, the pitcher will move behind third base or home plate on a base hit, depending on where he thinks the play will be made. While backing up, the pitcher will position himself near the stands to be in position to retrieve an overthrow and keep the runners from advancing an extra base.

Cripple Pitch — Refers to the situation where the pitcher is behind in the ball-strike count 3-0 or 3-1. To keep from walking the hitter, he has to come in with the pitch. Naturally, he cannot afford to be too fine with the pitch, thereby taking the chance of throwing a cripple pitch.

Long Reliever — Used in the early innings after the starting pitcher has been forced out of the game. His job is to hold the opposition for a few innings and give his club a chance to catch up.

Make 'em Hit your Pitch — There are runners on base in a clutch situation. The pitcher is ahead on the ball-strike count. In this situation, the pitching coach will remind him not to give the batter a good pitch to hit, but to "make 'em hit your pitch."

Middle Reliever — The middle man is called upon from about the fifth to the seventh innings. On most clubs, the middle reliever also functions as the third short reliever or second long reliever, depending on the size of the pitching staff.

Mix 'em Up — This is the pitching coach's reminder to the pitcher to vary the type and speed of his pitches to keep the hitters guessing. Keeping hitters off stride is the secret to effectiveness as a pitcher.

Off the Hook — When a pitcher leaves a game with his club behind in the score and the club rallies to tie or go ahead, the pitcher no longer can be charged with the loss and is "off the hook."

Rosin Bag — Small bag of powered rosin kept on the mound and used by the pitcher to improve his grip on the ball.

Setup Man — The short reliever who comes into a game with his club holding a lead and holds the opposition until the manager summons the short man or, as commonly referred to, the stopper. This may mean the setup man pitches to one batter or several batters. But regardless of how effective he has been, the stopper will be called on to pitch the ninth inning.

Southpaw —A left-handed pitcher. The name came about because most of the original ballparks were laid out with the first base line running almost east and west, resulting in the throwing arm of the left-hander coming from the south as he made the pitch.

Stopper — The money pitcher who is called on when the game is on the line to put down a budding rally and nail down a victory. Most stoppers are only called upon when their club is ahead in the score or tied. Because he could be called upon to pitch several days in a row, he must possess a rubber arm. Without the kind of short man who can be effective and consistent in tough situations, it's difficult for any club to win a pennant. Also, referred to as *closer* or *fireman*.

Warm-Up Pitches — A pitcher is allowed eight warm-up pitches before each inning or after coming into the game in relief. The one exception: in case of an injury to the pitcher, the relief pitcher may be allowed as much warm-up time as needed.

CATCHING

Crossed Up — What happens when the catcher signals for one type of pitch and the pitcher throws another. It occurs most often with a runner on second base and the catcher switches signs. Nothing upsets a catcher more than to be crossed up. There is a real physical risk when he expects one pitch and gets another.

Infield Drift — On pop-ups behind home plate, the rotation of the ball is back toward the playing field. To compensate for this infield drift, the catcher turns his back to the infield to catch the pop up. In this position, the ball is coming back toward him and is an easier play.

Strikeout, Throw Out — When the batter strikes out with less than two outs and the catcher throws out a runner trying to steal a base. Result: a double play.

Waste Pitch — Pitch called by the catcher that is purposely thrown out of the strike zone, usually on a no-ball, two-strike count, in an attempt to entice the batter to swing.

IN THE FIELD

Alley — The gap between the outfielders.

Around the Horn — A double play that goes from the third baseman to the second baseman to the first baseman has gone around the horn. The term also describes the action of throwing the ball around the infield after the first or second out is recorded and no one is on base.

Around to Right — Against a left-handed pull hitter or a right-handed opposite-field hitter, the outfielders move toward the right field side of the field. This position puts the left fielder in toward left-center field, the center fielder toward right-center field and the right fielder near the right field foul line. "Around to Left" would find the outfielders moving in the opposite direction.

Checking the Runner — When a base runner fails to touch a base as he heads to the next base, it is not the responsibility of the umpire to call attention to the runner's error. As far as the umpire is concerned there is no violation of the rules until the defensive team makes an appeal to the umpire and steps on the base that was missed. Once the play is over and the ball becomes "dead," the pitcher will put the ball in play, step back off the pitching rubber and throw to the baseman nearest the missed base. Once the base has been touched, the umpire will rule on the appeal.

Decoy — The Academy Award performance of either the second baseman or shortstop when the runner is running on the pitch (hit-and-run play) and the batter pops the ball into the air. If the runner fails to take a glance over his shoulder at the point the hitter makes contact with the ball, the infielder covering second will act like a ground ball has been hit to another fielder and a throw to second is imminent. If the fielder is successful in "decoying" the runner into continuing on toward second, the runner becomes an easy target for a double play once the fly ball is caught.

Fungo Practice — Before a game during batting practice, a coach uses a long, thin bat (fungo bat) and hits ground balls to the infielders in between batters taking practice cuts in the batting cage. The two circles to the right and left of home plate are where the coaches "fungo" balls to fielders during batting practice.

Hole — The area not covered by an infielder. The most prominent hole on the infield is the one between the third baseman and the short-stop. More balls travel through this hole than any other. When the shortstop ranges far to his right to field a grounder, he is said to be deep in the hole.

Infield Practice — Before the start of a game, the home club usually takes a 10-minute round of infield practice. The visiting club follows. During infield practice, each infielder has the opportunity to field several ground balls and make appropriate throws to first and second base.

Kick It Out — When a bunt or slowly hit ball rolls in foul terri-tory very close to the foul line and there is little chance of putting the batter out, the fielder should "kick it out" with a swipe of his glove, batting the ball away from the foul line. Once the ball is touched by a fielder in foul territory, the umpire will call the ball foul. The fielder's action insures the ball does not roll back into fair territory.

Knock It Down — Reminder from the bench that with a very important run on second base it's crucial for infielders to make every effort to keep the ball from going into the outfield. Knocking the ball down keeps it in the infield and prevents the runner from scoring.

Rundown Play — What occurs when a runner is caught between bases. The defense will try to get the runner moving back toward the base he came from. For instance, a runner trapped off first base on a pickoff move by the pitcher will break for second base. The first base-man delivers the ball to the shortstop. If the runner stops, the short-stop will run toward him with the ball to get him moving back toward first, then throws the ball to the first baseman for the tag. The field-ers receiving the throws during a rundown play must stay out of the baseline to avert a potential *obstruction play*.

There He Goes — When a runner on base breaks for the next base as the pitch is made, the fielder nearest the runner (along with teammates on the bench) will yell, "There he goes!" to inform the catcher the runner is running and allowing the catcher to prepare to throw to the appropriate base.

MANAGERIAL STRATEGY

Batting Coach — Coach assigned to work with the hitters. The batting coach will use video tapes to analyze a hitter's mechanics and offer tips for improvement. Most of the coach's efforts come during special batting practices for players needing additional instruction.

Bullpen Coach — Coach in charge of the bullpen during a game. Normally, this position is manned by a former professional catcher who can assist with warming up relief pitchers during the game and offer instruction to catchers during practice sessions.

Clubhouse Meeting — Before the first game of a series, the manager will assemble the players to go over the strengths and weaknesses of the opposing team. Each hitter in the lineup — his strengths and weaknesses against both left-handed and right-handed pitchers, running speed, where he is likely to hit certain pitches — is discussed. This information is used to plan defensive strategy. Also discussed are the strengths and accuracy of the opposing outfielders.

Ground Crew — Team hired to assist the groundskeeper prepare and maintain the playing field.

Lineup Card — A printed form in triplicate used by the manager to record the names and positions of the nine players selected to start the game. The order the names appear on the card is also the order in which the players will bat. Each manager keeps a copy as does the home plate umpire.

Pitching Coach — Coach responsible for the pitching staff. He helps the pitchers devise strategy, develop new pitches, correct flaws in delivery, and conditioning. During the game he talks with the pitcher about things he may or may not be doing and assist the manager in making decisions to remove a pitcher from the game.

Trainer — The manager's unsung hero. The trainer looks after the players' aches, pains and injuries, and keeps the manager informed on which players are able to perform. A good trainer can help a team on the field by keeping the players in the best possible condition and promptly treating injuries to keep them from getting worse.

UMPIRES AND RULES

Ball Bag — A small bag on the home plate umpire's belt in which six baseballs are kept to use any time a ball is fouled off or scuffed.

Indicator — A small, hand-held device used by the home plate umpire to help him keep track of balls, strikes, outs and runs scored. The official ball-strike count is the one shown on the umpire's indicator, not the scoreboard.

Mound Measuring Device — Device used by the *umpire-in-chief* to measure the height (no more than 10 inches) and slope (1 inch per foot from the front edge of the pitching rubber) of the pitching mound. This insures some conformity from one pitching mound to another, making it easier for pitchers to adjust.

Super Mud — Chalk-colored mud found along the banks of the Delaware River used by the umpires to dull the gloss on new baseballs without significantly changing the balls' color. Umpires apply super mud to approximately five dozen baseballs (eight dozen for a doubleheader) before each game.

Umpire-In-Chief — Umpire named by the league president to be the leader for each four-man umpiring crew. The chief umpire usually makes a final decision if two or more umpires have conflicting decisions on the same play, is responsible for deciding to play or not during inclement weather, and whether or not a game is to be forfeited.

AVERAGES, RECORDS AND AWARDS

K — In scoring, "K" designates a strikeout. The letter K was chosen because it is the last letter of the word struck. The letter S was not chosen because it might be confused with the letters SS used to signify the shortstop.

POSITION NUMBERING AND ABBREVIATIONS

Position	Position No.	Abbreviation
Pitcher	1	P
Catcher	2	C
First Base	3	1B
Second Base	4	2B
Third Base	5	3B
Shortstop	6	SS
Left Field	7	LF
Center Field	8	CF
Right Field	9	RF